Problem-Based Learning in the College Music Classroom

Edited by **Natalie Sarrazin**

THE COLLEGE AT BROCKPORT, STATE UNIVERSITY OF NEW YORK

Routledge
Taylor & Francis Group

NEW YORK AND LONDON

First published 2019
by Routledge
711 Third Avenue, New York, NY 10017

and by Routledge
2 Park Square, Milton Park, Abingdon, Oxon, OX14 4RN

Routledge is an imprint of the Taylor & Francis Group, an informa business

Library of Congress Cataloging-in-Publication Data
Names: Sarrazin, Natalie Rose, editor.
Title: Problem-based learning in the college
music classroom / edited by Natalie Sarrazin.
Description: New York: Routledge, 2018. | Includes index.
Identifiers: LCCN 2018013237 (print) | LCCN 2018016948 (ebook) |
ISBN 9781351265249 (ebook) | ISBN 9781138578166 (hardback) |
ISBN 9781138578173 (pbk.)
Subjects: LCSH: Music in universities and colleges. |
Music—Instruction and study. | Problem-based learning.
Classification: LCC MT18 (ebook) | LCC MT18 .P76 2018 (print) |
DDC 780.71/1—dc23
LC record available at https://lccn.loc.gov/2018013237

ISBN: 978-1-138-57816-6 (hbk)
ISBN: 978-1-138-57817-3 (pbk)
ISBN: 978-1-351-26524-9 (ebk)

Typeset in Minion Pro
by codeMantra

Contents

Foreword

I'll never forget the preface to Arnold Schoenberg's book *Theory of Harmony* (1911/1978). It begins with the words, "This book I have learned from my students." He offered a strategy of teaching that was a precursor to what we now call PBL. "Had I told [my students] merely what I know, then they would have known just that and nothing more." He continued by emphasizing that the goal of his teaching was to encourage students to search because the search for knowledge and understanding in and of itself was a process of learning. He wrote, "I hope my pupils will commit themselves to searching! Because they will know that one searches for the sake of searching. That finding, which is indeed the goal, can easily put an end to striving."

The collection of chapters in this book is about how a group of colleagues across the SUNY system embarked on a journey of creating projects and curriculum to move their students toward engagement. Their case studies range from music history and appreciation, ethnomusicology, music and movement, music theory to music education. I was in on this project from the beginning when I traveled to New York from Southern California (in the winter mind you!) to work with the SUNY professors on PBL techniques. The professors jumped in head first, openly and enthusiastically. They already understood that it was time to move away from pure lecturing. After all, in this day and age, students really don't need anyone to tell them "things" since they can look up any of the subject matter online via a simple Google search. After our multiday intensive workshops, each of the professors went back to their campuses and began the process of inventing, refining, implementing, and reflecting on their practices. As you'll read in the delightful stories and case studies within this book, each professor found a creative way to move their curricula goals forward, all with their students clearly at the center of engaged learning.

As you read through the chapters, also keep in mind that this process set the stage for collective impact. It brought together professors from across the vast SUNY system and supported them in their pedagogy; and through the publication of this book, connects their work for others to see as well. The work in each of the classrooms served to awaken interest and participation. Schoenberg also wrote in his preface to Theory of Harmony, "It should be clear that the teacher's first task is to shake up the pupil thoroughly." This book would make Schoenberg very happy. It certainly has that effect on me.

Merryl Goldberg
California State University San Marcos

Preface

This book was made possible by the support of two SUNY Innovative Instructional Technology Grants (IITG), which award proposals that offer fresh and new approaches to pedagogy. The first grant supported training, and the supplemental grant supported the publication of our work in this book. Given the lack of research into how PBL can impact music classes, this project allows pedagogical discovery and provides initial case studies in this area – work which coincided with the IITG's ideals and mission. Initial inspiration for the project came from Dr. Tony Dumas, at the College at Brockport, as he sought ways to innovate and engage students in his World Music course. From there, the project developed into a statewide SUNY event in which ten colleagues were invited to attend a weekend workshop on designing and implementing PBL, run by myself, Dr. Dumas – with guest speakers Chris Price and Dale Hartnett, from the Center for Excellence in Learning and Teaching at Brockport – Dr. Merryl Goldberg, an expert on Arts Integration, and other types of innovative pedagogical instruction who helped guide us through the nuances of applying this type of strategy in our classrooms.

Additional thanks go to Dr. Darwin Prioleau, Dean of the Arts Humanities and Social Sciences at Brockport, and P. Gibson Ralph, Chair of Theatre and Music Studies, for their institutional and moral support for the project.

Introduction

1

The Essence of Problem-Based Learning and Music

NATALIE SARRAZIN

This chapter introduces readers to a general history and background of Problem-Based Learning (PBLs), defining it within the context of learning theory in general. The chapter also gives an overview of the various types of PBLs, distinguishing between Project- and Problem-based learning and paying particular attention to the application of this method in higher education music classroom.

> To find out how to make knowledge when it is needed is the true end of the acquisition of education in school, not the information itself.
>
> J. and E. Dewey, *Schools of Tomorrow* (1915, p. 13)

~

Classrooms can be challenging places for both teachers and students, especially given the proliferation of technology in day-to-day life. In the context of easy access to information, lecturing and note taking seem almost quaint at this point. Videos and PowerPoint no longer effectively motivate or interest students, and even the most entertaining and dynamic professors have trouble holding a class's full attention. Students, with the world at their fingertips, eschew learning discrete facts. Names, dates, places, narratives, and spelling are readily available and no longer require student effort to retain these facts in their brains, and many experts agree that they shouldn't have to. Meanwhile, educators, finding themselves struggling to satisfy an increased demand in institutional assessment, might be tempted to "lower the bar" by relaxing course objectives or the number of assignments, hoping that students show measurable progress. Perhaps students are ahead of the curve and sense that a dramatic shift in pedagogical practice is needed. They often express resentment toward courses that demand rote memorization or "busy work" that encroaches on their time outside of class, as they try to balance their social lives and work responsibilities. Students also sense that devoting time to study outside of class results in a diminishing lack of returns for them – their efforts appear to be redundant considering pervasive information that duplicates the text or lectures, answers readily available via the Internet, and, of course, instructors whose pedagogical methods don't seem in sync with their lifestyles or needs. The cycle continues as professors sense this lack of learning enthusiasm and lament a lost spark of student enthusiasm for learning in general. Quick-fix panaceas to combat this curricular conundrum are hard to come by given the cataclysmic changes wrought by technologically oriented lifestyles. Professors wrangle with solutions – whether to include any and all technology and social media (e.g. smartphones, iClickers, Twitter), go back to basics, or something in between.

Since students are not likely to give up their access to information, or their desire for a more practical and applicable education to fit their lifestyles, any time soon, the most effective educational practices will accommodate these things as a way to enhance learning and not view them as an obstacle to learning. Effective education, according to many education reformers, requires a drastic rewrite of current practices which replaces what seems to be a trend toward superficial learning with a highly in-depth level of learning. Dr. David Helfand, Columbia University, for example, places an emphasis on the "process-based" nature of education and has worked for years on such a hands-on approach to education, where depth and process supersede breadth and product. He was instrumental in successfully implementing this at Quest University in Canada, where students take a single course every month in a curriculum that focuses on how disciplines function in the world at large rather than within the confines of an academic institution. Since most universities and colleges cannot accommodate a curriculum that requires that students take only one course for three and a half weeks, other methods that deliver the same experiential results are invaluable.

Problem-based Learning (PBL), therefore, might be a part of the solution. PBL is a practical teaching and learning approach that allows a similar, intense, hands-on experience within a traditional higher educational setting. One way to think about this approach given by Ross (1997) in an examination of the PBL curriculum is that "knowledge arises from working on a problem, rather than, as with problem-solving, being a prerequisite for working on a problem" (34–41). Rather than asking students to regurgitate facts, which would probably send students directly to their phones for an answer, PBL allows students to use their phones as sources of information in the process of problem-solving. In other words, the phone is not going to give them the answers anymore, cannot form the questions they need to ask, or can't identify the process they need to work through to find the solution. Students must divine this for themselves.

Despite the initial and prevalent use of the PBL approach in more professionally oriented disciplines such as medicine and science, the notion that there are problems to be solved in music classes as well has not caught on. Perhaps this is due to the territorial nature of people in music sub-specialty areas who wish to retain their specialization or due to the deeply imbedded belief across the arts in its intrinsic value or, put more colloquially, arts for art's sake. In this philosophy, art is separated from its more mundane and utilitarian functions and treated as worthy of study in and of itself. This approach remains a staunch underpinning for all of the art forms that perhaps preempts an exploration of the real-life application of PBL. After all, if students are appreciating music for music's sake, there is less of a need for further inquiry learning about the real-world mechanisms it takes to produce that art in the first place.

As the case studies in this book will show, however, music courses are uniquely situated to advance this effective pedagogical approach. It is possible not only to include PBL in almost every type of music course, but it also allows students in these courses to find a new level of interdisciplinarity for music – a place where music curricula rarely ever go. For example, students in a music theory class can analyze music performance at the level of gesture and nonverbal music behavior, or students in a music appreciation class become artistic directors of orchestras to discover and solve problems faced on a day-to-day basis by people in those positions.

PBL aims directly at the heart of student engagement. Even in music classes such as applied, theory, and music education, which we perceive to be more participatory than other courses, students can remain aloof and removed from the material. As these case studies will demonstrate, PBLs encourage "outside of the classroom" thinking, requiring them to connect academic learning to real-life situations. PBL is based on high levels of student input, encouraging them to draw on and integrate several knowledge-based content areas, thereby becoming more active participants in their own education. PBL, when applied in a general education curriculum, allows students to see the connections across disciplines from their first year through to their capstone experiences.

PBL: From Memorization to Application

PBL is hailed as one of the most effective instructional methods conceived in education, one in which an engaged learning approach addresses crucial areas of concern such as content retention, problem-solving skills, higher-order thinking, self-directed and life-long learning, and student self-perception and confidence (Hung et al., 2008, 486). In the introduction of their book *The Challenge of Problem-based Learning*, Boud and Feletti state that PBL is the most significant innovation in education of the professions for many years (1997, 1), while Maudsley notes its usefulness as a tool for epistemological reform in higher education (1999, 178).

PBL began in the medical field in the 1950s to train physicians (Barrows, 2009/1986). The thought behind its use was its effectiveness in clinical contexts, which would aid in future recall, and to encourage medical education away from rote memorization and "fragmented biomedical knowledge" and "equip students with clinical problem-solving and lifelong learning skills (Albanese and Mitchell, 1993; Barrows, 1996). Although initially geared toward this profession, PBL has expanded over the years to include others such as architecture, social work, business, and legal training. For example, PBL usage in fields such as law, engineering, and other professions occurred in the 1990s, while Barrows and Kelson (1993) were instrumental in introducing PBL into K-12 curricula as well (Hung et al., 2008).

The PBL approach has eventually made its way into higher and even secondary education as well. There are dozens of resources for PBL in elementary and secondary education – sites like edutopia.org, bie.org (Buck Institute for Education), and educationcloset.com. Bie.org is one of the largest and most comprehensive websites for learning about PBL and is highly recommended. The material in this book expands the core tenets of PBL to include the college music classroom – exploring its design, implementation, materials, methods, challenges, and outcomes in survey- and topic-based music courses that integrate general education content while encouraging students to think creatively and develop flexible solutions to large-scale issues and problems – skills essential for success in the 21st century.

An Exploration of Music Courses and PBL

PBL is described by Barrows as the "learning which results from the process of working towards the understanding of, or resolution of a problem" (Barrow and Tamblyn, 1980). Although the idea of PBL is implemented in secondary (7–12) music education circles, music education's use of PBL is at a nascent stage of exploration and development. Currently, PBL advice and tips appear on blogs and are presented as the latest new ideas in music education, without much in the way of depth, literature, or training as to its implementation. Additionally, the music education approach follows that of a Dewey-inspired, student-centered learning (e.g. Hayden, 2015 "Personalized Learning through Problem-based Music"; Miller, 2012 "Use PBL to innovate in the Music Classroom"). While student-centered learning is certainly a goal of any PBL strategy, models for implementing PBL in higher education courses allow a much more intensive experience, not only at the individual level but more importantly at the group/collaborative learning level where college students who study different majors and minors can share their experiences and expertise, thus allowing a richer and more varied learning experience.

The book will address two main shortcomings in the existing literature on PBL. First, until now, no book has directly focused on a *music* application of PBL. The idea that music study can address the real world and contribute to issues and problems is consistently overlooked. The case studies in this book address a range of applications, from more abstract to concrete applications, which may help to answer real-world questions and have real-world consequences. This, above all, situates the study of music as a significant contributor to seeing and understanding the world.

Second, literature on the subject has concentrated on practical applications while largely ignoring the challenges and complexities of the processes involved in PBLs. The chapters in this book will address these complexities through tested case studies in which instructors elaborate in detail on the curricular and student learning outcomes (SLO) changes, timeline creation and execution, assessment and rubric design, and numerous other details and adjustments. One of the main questions each instructor asked themselves is how they could successfully apply PBL to their current classroom without too much disruption or change. Music as a subject and discipline has many facets – theoretical, applied, historical, social, and performative, all of which require different teaching approaches and skill sets. Can PBL accommodate all of these areas?

In addition, not all of PBL projects are successful, and authors will focus on the varying results of their successes and failures and thoughtfully reflect on what might be improved along the way.

Book Outline

This volume demonstrates the application of PBL across many music disciplines such as theory, history, applied skills, and so forth, as well as in a range of class types, from large survey courses to smaller, upper-division special topics courses. The book begins with a general introduction to PBL, including appropriate literature review and a general review of its use in other college subjects. This introductory chapter will then present general strategies for using the PBL approach in various college music classrooms.

Nine case studies are then presented, each fitting into four subsections: Music History and Appreciation, Ethnomusicology, Music and Movement, and Music Theory and Education, with two to three case studies in each subsection. Each case study addresses a different application of PBL in music courses, providing the reader with a wide range of instructional design, assessment, examples, and strategies. Finally, the book concludes with a chapter on best practices, guidelines, and assessment, in which the editor reviews the outcomes of the case studies and provides an overview on the efficacy of the different approaches.

Main Themes and Objectives

The major objective of this book is to provide examples of concrete, classroom-tested PBL for use by music instructors across a range of higher education music courses. The Objective of the book focuses on tailoring the following to college music classes specifically:

- Introducing group work and collaboration in music
- Familiarizing the reader with Problem-based strategies and designs
- Including examples of useful materials
- Providing a means of assessment and evaluation of PBL work

Since PBL in higher education music courses is relatively rare in the literature, the book's case studies will outline ideas for developing and implementing different types of PBLs.

Sources for Problem-Based Learning

As of now, there are no books and few articles on the subject of PBL in a college music classroom, nor are there books on PBL in the music classroom at any level. Although there may be a scattered article on music here and there, no article focusing on PBL and music appears in *The Interdisciplinary Journal of Problem-Based Learning* in the ten years since its inception.

Most texts on PBL can be separated into several categories; earlier ones addressing its application in the medical field (1980s–2000) and later ones addressing PBL in general. The latter present PBL's application and impact on higher education, including descriptions, problem construction, obstacles to implementation, and ventures into general higher education needs (e.g. administration, facilitation, and evaluation).

Scattered throughout the years are texts that include forays into other subjects areas, but most of these are still science related given the acceptance of the case study in teaching and learning. A few of the relevant texts can be found below.

There are several general texts that introduce PBLs which are useful to understanding this subject. Duch, Groh, and Allen's (Eds.) (2001) "The power of Problem-Based learning: A practical 'how to' for teaching undergraduate courses in any discipline" is an excellent introduction to the subject. Based on a National Science Foundation grant to help revitalize undergraduate education in science, technology, engineering and mathematics (STEM) classes, the book addresses some of the initial questions of implementation, including obstacles, challenges, designing materials, and reflecting on how the process can be developed, implements, and its effects on the subject. To that end, the text includes pragmatic strategies for including administrative support, developing a structure to initiate PBL its facilitation and problem writing. The book contains several case studies in a range of fields, but most, not surprisingly, are STEM-based (e.g. nursing, biochemistry, physics, and technology). The humanities are underrepresented, and music is not represented in this collection.

Another general text, Savin-Baden and Major's "Foundations of Problem-based Learning" (2004) fills in the history and learning theory gap in the subject, providing the reader with definitions, background on PBL, implementation, further applications to include culture and diversity, and, most importantly, assessment and evaluation of PBL. There are very few case studies included, however, and no mention of implementation in a music classroom or in any other arts-based curriculum.

Barrett and Moore's "New Approaches to Problem-Based Learning: Revitalising Your Practice in Higher Education" (2011) is similar to Duch's PBL listed above, and it focuses on PBL's impact on higher education but provides one of the most comprehensive texts on the subject. It includes an investigation of all of the participants involved, developing learning initiatives, how PBL enhances student capabilities, and ways of sustaining PBL. In a creative twist, the last chapter reveals the PBL process by which the book was written. Again, this text is a general overview of the PBL process and does not focus on any one particular subject.

In terms of specific music-related PBL studies, Yang's 2014 article "Teaching Music History at Hong Kong Baptist University: Problem-Based Learning and Outcome-based Teaching and Learning" is one of the only music articles published that presents the implementation of PBL in a college music classroom. This very short paper is primarily Yang's reflection on PBL in her class, in which she shares several problems presented to a music history class, along with the several issues and a general evaluation of the process. The problems she presents to the class, however, are not all suitable for PBL. Out of the three given, only one is problem-Based, while the other two are project-based. Problem- and Project-based learning are commonly confused by instructors trying out this strategy. The definitions and distinctions are given below.

Problem-Based Learning as Inquiry: An Overview

PBL is a type of inquiry-based learning pedagogy. According to H. S. Barrows, one of the leading scholars on PBL, the term itself does not refer to any one type of teaching method but varies according to context (Barrows, 2009). An inquiry approach to learning is certainly not new and, in fact, is thousands of years old. More recent manifestations are rooted in constructivist theories of education, primarily Vygotsky, Piaget, and Dewey, which stress active inquiry and discovery as opposed to student memorization. The educational philosopher John Dewey was highly critical of learning that did not emphasize process and critical thinking and instead relied on fact memorization. One of the most well-known works of PBL, rooted in Dewey's 19th-century philosophy and 18th-century applications in architecture and engineering, and the early 20th-century progressive education movement, formed the basis for William Kilpatrick's essay entitled "The Project Method" (1918). Kilpatrick's essay describes the basic features of PBL: child-centered in that students solve problems with the teacher as facilitator. Savery looks at the constructivist roots of PBL and credits Barrows' contribution (1985, 1986, 1992) as one of the best examples of it.

In general, all types of PBLs are similar in that they, first and foremost, involve a student-centered approach to learning and involve inquiry or discovery learning. Often, two types of learning labels, which are often interchanged, are Project-based and Problem-Based. According to John Larmer at the Buck Institute of Learning (bie.org), both Project- and Problem-Based Learning as types of inquiry-based learning involve a central question as the prompt for student learning. PBL had its roots in the 1960s discovery learning phase and emerged in medical science as a viable and primary method for case-based student learning as mentioned above. PBL, therefore, is a type of Project-based Learning, along with many other types of learning. Problem- and Project-based Learning overlap, but there are several distinctions. Both types of PBLs

- Are student-centered
- Focus on an open-ended question or task
- Provide authentic applications of content and skills
- Build 21st-century success skills
- Emphasis student independence and inquiry
- Are longer and more multifaceted than traditional lessons or assignments (adapted from Edutopia.org).

The similarities after this point continue in that both can be multi-subject or single-subject, with Project-based lending itself more toward multi-subject. They can be long or short, with Project-based tending toward a longer length. They both follow prescribed steps toward the outcome, and both can utilize real-life or fictitious scenarios, with Project-based focusing more on real-life problems. The major difference is in the final outcome. Project-based Learning requires the creation of a product or performance, whereas Problem-Based "products" may be concrete or in the form of a proposed solution or presentation.

Jumping In: Designing a Music-Related PBL (Problem or Project)

In a sense, developing a driving question for a PBL is similar to the Socratic method of inquiry-based education. It might be effective to think of the project from the end point and work backward to that initial question. For example, decide what you want students to end up knowing by the conclusion of the class, and then deduce what they might need to do in order to get there.

There are several excellent sources that outline how to design a non-course-specific PBL. Websites such as Edutopia and the Buck Institute for Education (BIE) highlight the preparation process to create a PBL. Even if they're not directly dealing with music as a subject, the sites provide an excellent starting point for thinking about the scope, parameters, and assessment of a PBL.

Essential Project Design Elements (Adapted from bie.org for use in College Music Classes)

Table 1.1 includes the two significant components of the PBL process for teachers and students found in Larmer et al., *Setting the Standard for Project Based*

Learning: A Proven Approach to Rigorous Classroom Instruction (ASCD 2015). The column on the left, Teaching Practices, concerns the teacher's input and creation efforts, including pedagogical scaffolding, and perspective on the overall process and expectations. The column on the right, Design Elements, concerns the student engagement with the project, including their expectations and input.

Teaching Practices also begins to address the change in control the instructor should expect. PBL requires that the teacher reconceptualize the standard teaching role of lecturer and relinquish a fair amount of classroom control

Table 1.1

PBL Teaching Practices	PBL Design Elements
Design and Plan Teacher-created project and implementation plan – may have some degree of student input	**Challenging Problem or Question** Problem is meaningful and worth solving, appropriately challenging for the group, and fueled by a driving question
Align to Standards Teachers use standards; addressing key areas of the subject to be included	**Sustained Inquiry** Active process: Students generate their own questions and answers, seek and use appropriate resources
Build the Culture Teacher promotes student independence, growth, open-ended inquiry, collaboration, and quality	**Authenticity** Project has real-world implications, requires real-world tools and processes, and is of interest to students concerns and identities
Manage Activities Teacher organizes classes, schedules, deadlines, and resources	**Student Voice and Choice** Students have input into the project, choices, work processes, and use of time
Scaffold Student Learning Teacher employs a variety of lessons, tools, and strategies to support project goals	Reflection Students take time to reflect on the learning process itself and the project's design
Assess Student Learning Teachers assess understanding and knowledge, including self- and peer assessment	**Critique and Revision** Students give and receive feedback on their work
Engage and Coach Teachers engage in learning and creating along with students and identify student needs: skill-building, redirection, encouragement, etc.	**Public Product** Students demonstrate what they learn through a presented product (to people outside of the classroom)

Source: Larmer et al., Setting the Standard for Project Based Learning: A Proven Approach to Rigorous Classroom Instruction (ASCD 2015).

over to the students. This is counterintuitive to traditional instructional behavior and does take some getting used to.

Regardless of the format and process of PBL, the essential goal is the development of critical-thinking and problem-solving skills, collaboration, and personal goal-setting and time management for students – in other words, independent, self-, or group-directed learning.

How Do I Know If My Activity Is a PBL?

PBLs vary widely according to discipline, approach, student learning needs, teacher preparation, and a host of other factors. It is easy to question whether what you've developed falls under the category of PBL. To assess your proposed activity, Charlin et al. developed a set of criteria to determine if it qualifies as PBL through three core principles:

1. The problem acts as a stimulus for learning
2. It is an educational approach, not an isolated instructional technique
3. It is a student-centered approach, and the four criteria concerning their effect on student learning are as follows:
   - Active processing of information
   - Activation of prior knowledge
   - Meaningful context
   - Opportunities for elaboration/organization of knowledge (2009)

Developing a Musically Driven Question

In a true- or open-inquiry approach, students would develop their own questions to answer. This is always an option for any educator. However, for purposes of assessment and comparison, having one guiding question is also helpful. What constitutes a good driving question for a music PBL?

Considering the list given above, the problem must act as a stimulus for learning, where further learning is generated not only by the question itself but also by the process of answering and investigating answers to the question. If there is a direct answer available to the question, there is no room for discovery and inquiry. For example, the question "what are cadences?" would yield a very specific answer. Asking the question "how have cadences changed over time?" allows much more room for exploration.

Instructional and performance techniques are highly prevalent in music given its applied aspects, and it is easy to conflate an isolated skill building instructional technique with one that is considered part of a larger educational approach. For example, asking students to create a harmonic progression using boom whackers is not a PBL activity, whereas asking the value of boom whackers to teach music theory would be.

Criteria for creating good PBL questions in music are the same as those for any subject. Questions should be provocative and interesting, allow for rigorous inquiry and debate, and be purposefully vague and open-ended.

The following might be some examples of non-course-specific PBL music questions:

- What is music?
- What limits musical creativity?
- Can music be taught?
- Is music a universal language?
- What is improvisation?
- Should governments fund the arts?

More course-specific real-world questions might have students complete the following:

- Produce a musical with no budget
- Create a concert series for a particular demographic or with a specific repertoire
- Discover how musicians communicate (nonverbally) during performance

One excellent online resource is *Engaging Students: Essays in Music Pedagogy Vol. 2* which focuses on student-centered learning approaches. The contribution by Phil Duker offers an engaging range of PBL examples for the College music theory classroom, including analysis, composition and part-writing, and improvisation. Some of the more engaging problems include being a forensic musicologist and handling an eccentric wedding request.

Many questions have an interdisciplinary aspect to them as well, something covered by Merryl Goldberg (see Chapter 2 in this volume).

Elements in the Teaching Practices list are self-explanatory and flexible in that they can be used for any type of classroom from K-College. For higher education, small adjustments in emphasis can be made in the "Align to Standards" section, which, in higher education speak, refers to student learning outcomes rather than the Common Core Standards which are applicable to primary and secondary education.

Scheduling class time for PBL is another concern, as it can usually take multiple classes or up to the whole semester. Relinquishing class time and deciding how much class time requires pre-planning and thought. What is the balance between time spent on lecture and problem-solving? How many classes or weeks will be devoted to the activity itself? The assessment? Follow-up?

Although this text cannot answer all of these questions, case studies of both types of PBLs and their solutions included in this volume demonstrate the great variety and flexibility in this type of inquiry-based education and its possible application in the college music classroom.

Bibliography

Albanese, Mark, and Mitchell, Susan. "Problem-Based Learning: A Review of Literature on Its Outcomes and Implementation Issues." *Academic Medicine* 68, no. 1 (1993): 52–81.

Barrows, Howard S. "A Taxonomy of Problem-Based Learning Methods." *Medical Education* 20, no. 6 (1986): 481–86.

Barrows, Howard. S., and Kelson, A. *"Problem-Based Learning in Secondary Education and the Problem-Based Learning Institute" (Monograph)*. Springfield, IL: Southern Illinois University School of Medicine, 1995: 1–5.

Barrows, Howard S., and Kelson A. M. *Problem-Based Learning: A Total Approach to Education. Monograph*. Springfield, IL: Southern Illinois University School of Medicine, 1993.

Barrows, Howard S., and Robyn M. Tamblyn. *Problem-Based Learning: An Approach to MEDICAL Education*. New York, NY: Springer, 1980.

Boud, David, and Grahame Feletti. *The Challenge of Problem-Based Learning*. London: Kogan Page, 1997.

Charlin, Bernard, Mann, Karen, and Hansen, Penny. "The Many Faces of Problem-Based Learning: A Framework for Understanding and Comparison." *Medical Teacher* 20, no. 4 (2009): 323–30.

Dewey, J. and Dewey, E. *Schools of Tomorrow*. Literary Licensing. Boston, MA: Dutton and Company, 2014 (1915).

Duch, Barbara J., Groh, Susan E., and Deborah E. Allen. *The Power of Problem-Based Learning a Practical "How To" for Teaching Undergraduate Courses in any Discipline*. Vancouver: Access and Diversity, Crane Library, University of British Columbia, 2001.

Hayden, Michael. Personalized Learning through Problem-Based Music. December 1, 2015. https://nafme.org/personalized-learning-through-project-based-music/. Retrieved February 28, 2017.

Hung, Woei, Johanssen, David, and Liu, Rude. "Problem Based Learning." In J. M. Spector, J. G. van Merrienboer, M. D. Merrill, and M. Driscoll (eds.) *Handbook of Research on Educational Communications and Technology*, 3rd ed. New York: Lawrence Erlbaum Associates, 2008, 485–506. Retrieved March 13, 2017.

Kilpatrick, W. H. The Project Method. *Teachers College Record* 19, (1918): 319–335.

Knoll, M. "I Had Made a Mistake: William H. Kilpatrick and the Project Method." *Teachers College Record* 112, (2012): 1–45.

Maudsley, G. "Do We All Mean the Same Thing by "Problem-Based Learning"? A Review of the Concepts and a Formulation of the Ground Rules." *Academic Medicine* 74, no. 2 (1999): 178–85.

Miller, Andrew. Use PBL to Innovate the Music Classroom, 2012. www.edutopia.org/blog/project-based-learning-music-andrew-miller. Retrieved February 25, 2017.

Ross, Bob. "Towards a Framework for Problem-Based Curricula," In Boud, David, and Grahame Feletti (eds.) *The Challenge of Problem-Based Learning*. London: Kogan Page, 1997 (1991), 28–35.

Savery, J., and Duffy, T. "Problem-Based Learning: An Instructional Model and its Constructivist Framework." *Educational Technology*, 35/5 (1995): 31–38.

Resources

Duker, Phil. Problem-Based Learning in Music Theory Classes. http://flipcamp.org/engaging students2/essays/duker.html

Engaging Students: Essays in Music Pedagogy, Vol 2. http://flipcamp.org/engagingstudents2/index.html

Edutopia. https://www.edutopia.org/blog/pbl-vs-pbl-vs-xbl-john-larmer

PBL Video Archive (primary and secondary education). http://archive.pbl-online.org/video/video2.htm

2
Teaching and Learning in Higher Education Music Classes: It Don't Mean a Thing If It Ain't Got That Swing

MERRYL GOLDBERG

In this chapter, Merryl Goldberg contextualizes Project-based Learning by asking us to examine teaching and learning as a process of engagement before anything else and then reexamining the concept of music – first as text and then as an interdisciplinary tool. Above all, she reframes the divide in music between the ideas of technique versus creativity, a foil often used to justify and discredit music disciplines and pedagogies. She rounds out the chapter with mindfulness – an approach to learning that involves self-reflection and thought behind effective learning.

~

Learning by doing, active learning, or what some call Project-based learning, engages students as active participants in the learning process. Some of my earliest memories of learning in school were when I was actively engaged. I'll never forget flag day (June 14th) because each and every class at my school, McKay elementary school in Beverly, Massachusetts, would learn a song and sing it on the steps of our school. I especially remember second grade and the day we made butter. Our teacher, Mrs. Simmons, came to class with a glass jar half-filled with cream inside of it. She said each one of us would be having a turn at shaking the jar of cream, because after we did so, there would be a surprise. We sat upright in our desks, all neatly in rows, awaiting our turn which meant we would shake shake shake the jar. Each child shook about 25 times or so and then passed the jar to the person behind us. After 35 kids or so shook the jar passing it up and down the rows of our desks, the teacher opened the jar, and lo and behold, magic: we had transformed the cream into butter! Next, she put some of that butter onto Ritz crackers for each of us to try. I feel like it was yesterday! And, that butter was delicious.

My second-grade cream-shaking experience was an example of being involved. Not only were we actively engaged as learners, but the anticipation of what was going to happen heightened our curiosity and excitement. Nowadays, when I ask my students what they remember from school, inevitably they recall something they did, or a teacher who made an impression by paying attention to them. Rarely, if ever, will a student remember passive learning experiences such as doing worksheets. Instead, students remember being in a play, or going on a field trip, or a big art project. Project-based learning, the emphasis throughout this book, puts students on the road to active engagement. This chapter seeks to place the notion of Project-based learning within a broader context as well as situate it within the Higher Education music classroom.

When I was an undergraduate at New England Conservatory (NEC) of Music in Boston in the late 1970s and 1980s, I had a wide variety of teachers with different teaching styles. I had a theory teacher who encouraged our sight-singing abilities by challenging us to sing a page full of numbers from the phone book each day as practice. I also had a theory teacher who literally read to us from Arnold Schoenberg's *Theory of Harmony* text. That class was not very inspiring; though, I did come out of it with a very funny story. One day, I was sitting in class beside the piano. I had had a gig the night before and was pretty tired. Our teacher began reading from the text, and, as it would happen, I drifted off. In fact, I fell asleep. Some of my classmates witnessed this but were helpless because I was too out of reach for them to poke me. Well, I didn't fall over on the piano, but when the teacher asked me to play an example and I proved unresponsive, he came over and banged the heck out of the piano! I jumped, everyone laughed, including the teacher, and we all enjoyed the awkward moment. Our teacher was well aware of his limitations! In fact, the following week he sneaked in a pair of Groucho Marx glasses and as he was reading slowly looked up and gave us all another chuckle.

I had another teacher at NEC, Jim Hoffmann, who was in stark contrast to my harmony teacher. Jim Hoffmann was a brilliant Project-based educational innovator. I took several classes from him and continued to study with him through my graduate studies at Harvard, where he acted as a reader for my doctoral dissertation. Jim was also a wonderful composer, and I had the privilege of premiering many of his new works. His classes still inspire me as I develop projects for my own classes.

One class of his was an absolute standout: his 20th-century theory class. In this class, we studied composers including Stravinsky, Schoenberg, Babbit, Copeland, and Bartok. We studied scores, listened to music, examined the techniques, and then each week were charged with composing a small piece in the style of the particular composer we were studying. Our compositions had to be scored for the instrumentation of our fellow classmates so that each composition could be – and was – performed during class. The compositions gave each of us a tangible way to delve into the styles of the composers and an opportunity to demonstrate our understanding of the styles in a very tangible, creative manner. The compositions also served as an assessment tool for Jim (and the rest of us) as an indication of each student's understanding of the class material.

In teaching and learning, one thing is always for certain: if your class swings, you've got a great chance of students being engaged, curious, and involved. More importantly, you have the chance to set the stage for authentic learning to take place. One of the things that makes the learning of music through innovative project based learning stand out is that music in and of itself can be compelling in the realm of pedagogy. Unlike other subject content areas, the study of music can provide both a process through which students grapple with content (such as theory), and it is also a repository of content representing humanity's existence.

The process of art in the broader sense includes learning-specific skills known as technique, such as the technique of contour drawing in visual art, playing a musical instrument in tune as a musician, or projecting your voice as an actor. At the same time that technique underlies the artistic process, the making of music or other arts would not occur if there were not also an engagement of the imagination and creativity. A wonderful musician not only plays technically well, but she also interprets a piece of music in order to present it. The balance of technique with creativity provides the foundation for making art or playing music. Furthermore, as woven into a process of learning, the making of music can provide a teacher with tools to assess students' learning.

Art as Text – Arts Integration – Arts Education

The role of music in the context of what is called arts integration in teaching and learning is extensive and holds great potential for students as learners, and for teachers, in engaging students. As the focus of this book is Project-based learning specifically in music in Higher Education, the next part of this chapter sets the broader context of this work.

Music and art as text: All arts have a unique role in humanity as a document of events, emotions, history, culture, and ideas. Arts as Text places the focus on the arts as source material. Arts provide us with tangible reflections, documentation, and responses to the world, events, emotions, and experiences. When we examine art works closely, we are reading them. In music, if we are reading scores, we are literally reading music, but music as text refers more specifically to how we interpret meaning, feelings, emotions, and images through listening. In cultures such as Australian Aboriginal culture, music even is the key to mapping and geography. Music as text offers immense possibilities as we approach Project-based learning and active listening/learning.

Music in arts integration: Arts integration is an accepted tool for teaching and learning from kindergarten through Higher Education. Arts integration focuses on a process of learning by engaging arts-based strategies to integrate learning in the arts with other subjects. What is unique to arts integration is the attention on the process of learning in the arts to engage discipline learning outside of the arts, such as literacy, math, science, or social studies. In this category, the phrases "learning through the arts" and "learning with the arts" are commonplace. The Kennedy Center's definition for arts integration is "Arts integration is an approach to teaching in which students construct and demonstrate understanding through an art form. Students engage in a creative process, which connects an art form and another subject and meets evolving objectives in both."

Arts education commonly refers to learning in the disciplines of the arts: visual arts, music, dance, theater, and media arts, as subjects in and unto themselves. According to state and federal educational guidelines – each and every child is required to have an education in and about the arts. Learning music by focusing in on it as a discipline onto itself is the essence of music education.

Digging a Little Deeper

Let's dig into these concepts a bit more. In teaching and learning, one thing is always for certain: students are at the core of everything we do. I remember first really thinking about the importance of framing teaching and learning as a relationship while studying with Eleanor Duckworth at the Harvard Graduate School of Education (I would eventually become one of her teaching assistants). Eleanor had us read David Hawkin's *The Informed Vision* (1974) in which he framed teaching and learning as a three-way relationship between "I, thou, it." "I" is the teacher, "thou" the student, and the "it" is the content. While that framing of teaching and learning as a three-way relationship has worked for me for many years, I've come to realize that there is one big missing piece. Process is fundamental aspect of how we learn. And, the teachers who understand this use a process – Project-based learning as an example, as a bridge connecting content, student, and teacher.

One of the things that makes art so compelling in the realm of pedagogy is that it is both a process through which students grapple with content, and it is a repository of content representing humanity's experiences. A wonderful musician not only plays technically well, but she also interprets a piece of music in order to present it. The balance of technique with creativity provides the foundation for making art, as well as reflecting on it as an audience or viewer.

Music (Arts) as Text

To illustrate the power of Music as Text, we delve directly into active learning. I like to demonstrate music as text. To do so, I either perform for students live or have them listen closely to a piece of music I choose. I ask two simple questions as students listen to a piece of music. The two questions are as follows: 'What do you notice', and 'What do you wonder'? These two questions go a long way in learning in many contexts! In this particular context, the learning centers on historical and cultural connections, form, mode, rhythms, melody, and harmony. In addition, the example brings out curiosity concerning learning by ear versus learning through reading, as well as the role of improvisation in performing.

Since I am comfortable as a performer, I like to perform live. And, I can't say enough for providing students the opportunity to experience live music – especially since they are music students(!) or experience any of the performing arts for that matter. If I am doing this exercise for nonmusicians, then I get in front of the class or auditorium and introduce myself. However, I do not give away the name of the instrument or the kind of music I'm performing. Nor do I mention anything about the person accompanying me. If I am in a music class, I still hold back and say nothing – I simply launch into the tune.

My go-to piece of music to play for this exercise is from the genre of music called "klezmer" music, which is eastern European Yiddish music. The piece I play "Broiges Tanz" literally means "angry dance" and has a simple two-chord repetitive accompaniment of Dm and A7. Before I play, I ask students to keep two lists – one of what they notice about the music itself, its form, what it sounds like, or what it reminds them of (if anything). I also suggest they notice things about the way I play or interactions between myself and the other musician. I also ask them to make a second list of what they wonder; what they wonder about the music, about the musicians, about how we play, etc. Remember, I give them no background on myself, the instruments, or the piece at this point.

Then, I play. I take out my soprano saxophone, count off the beats, and play the piece. I learned the piece by ear from an old recording, and I play it without any music in front of me. The piece has a strong rhythm, with what in Yiddish is called "krechts" a sliding, groaning quality, similar to the opening clarinet line on Gershwin's Rhapsody in Blue. The form of the piece is AABB and repeats over and over, though I never play the melody exactly the same. If you can imagine a modest tempo dance scene from Fiddler on the Roof, you're on the right track.

After I play, I ask the question "what did you notice?" Hands pop up immediately each time I do this whether its kindergarteners, middle school kids (and that says a lot right there!) through to in-service teachers, administrators, or music majors. I often follow up with clarifying questions to further under-stand what they've latched onto. Among the things they notice:

- The music sounds "Egyptian," "Aladdin-like," or something from Fiddler on the Roof. Some people will say, "I can imagine a snake coming out of a basket." Some people will correctly guess it is klezmer. I follow up on all these guesses with "What about the music do you think makes it sound that way versus a country and western tune or an Irish jig?!" Often, a richness of description un-folds here.
- "The music sounds like you could dance to it." Again, I'll get them to try to describe why it sounds dance-like. This will often bring in great music vocabulary including the notion of rhythm and form.
- Students will remark on the interactions I have with the other mu-sician including noticing we look at each other, we have "secret" signals where we exchange clues to tempo, dynamics (volume) or repeats. Students will also remark on the physicality of our playing.

Once we have exhausted the things that they notice (or I cut them off!), we go into "What do you wonder?" This is where the magic begins to flow for me, as I can see the curiosity and engagement build. In encouraging won-der questions, the teacher can enable her or his students to set the stage for a year's worth of learning. Among the things that folks typically wonder with the klezmer tune are the following:

- What kind of music is this?
- Where did it come from?
- How did you learn to play it?
- Have you two ever played together before?
- How long did it take to learn the piece?
- What is the title of the song?
- When was it performed?
- How much do you practice?
- How long have you played?
- How did you rehearse?
- Is there improvisation?
- Why aren't you using [written] music?

Fortunately, I am able to address most if not all of the questions! And, in doing so, we have touched on social studies, geography, immigration, history, cul-ture, as well as musical concepts including practice, improvisation, learning and playing by ear, performance, embellishments, and musical motivation, all the while using or introducing music vocabulary. This exercise sets the stage for students' curiosity. I find that if students are curious – the stage is set for learning.

With this simple activity, students themselves can come up with intriguing questions, and a good part of teaching plays out on its own.

Music (Arts) Integration

Arts Integration takes many forms, from learning through the arts, to learning with arts, to making art, and to reviewing and evaluating art. Examples of learning through the arts would include (but are by no means limited to) acting out the metamorphosis of a butterfly in order to understand it, studying a painting from a mathematical perspective in order to build mathematical skills, becoming characters in a reading text, or creating puppets to explore events in history. Applied to the music classroom, my earlier example of Jim Hoffmann's use of composition is a wonderful example integrating music to learn theory! Other integration of music would be to create mathematical formulas in sounds, create raps or chants to relay information concerning historical events, or even creating sound pieces such as Vivaldi's Four Seasons.

In arts integration, the arts are a tool for teaching and learning. At the same time, arts integration is also about teaching the arts in and of themselves. In any subject of study, understanding is key to learning. Thus, using the example from Jim's class, if he were to have lectured to us about the various 20th-century composer's styles and we took a test about them, all Jim would really know would be if we could repeat back what he had told us. However, by engaging us in composing in the style of each composer, he knew at the very least we were working with the ideas. And, from our compositions and performances, he could evaluate the extent to which they understand the concept (or don't understand).

Music (Arts) Education

Arts Education: It's the law! Truly. According to the federal guidelines for education and most state mandates, the arts, e.g. music, visual art, dance, theater, and media arts, are required subjects within the curriculum. Unfortunately, neither the feds nor do most states have "arts education police" monitoring for compliance. Sadly, as a result of years of waning accessibility to the arts, especially among students in high-poverty settings, many students enter college with little to no exposure to the arts, putting them at a disadvantage in terms of college and career readiness.

Learning in and about music includes learning "how tos" – i.e. skills and techniques such as scales, intonation, and dynamics. It also includes learning about how music and its place in historical and cultural contexts. Ideally, and per the law, students are entitled to discipline-specific classes in music and in the other arts. Sometimes people talk about arts education as "arts for arts' sake." I tend to shy away from the notion of arts for art's sake in the sense that arts are rarely (if ever) without content or created in a bubble. Even when an artist like myself engages in practicing (in my case, practicing the saxophone), it is because we might simply have an immeasurable need to play, or draw, or dance. The practice usually brings us toward some end or brings us further in our art making. In fact, engaging in practice teaches us something about grit, perseverance, and discipline. It might also teach us something about the practice of mindfulness.

Mindfulness – Learning from the Future

To round out this chapter, I'm going to bring us once again back to my 20th-century theory class. One of the most interesting things about learning by or through composing is that each of us as students invented something we had never created or even imagined prior to the exercise. In some ways, we were learning by inventing – or learning "from the future." It is odd to think about learning in such a fashion, but it is exactly what we were doing. In order to learn, we had to invent a new composition. No one could tell us exactly what to do or how to compose it – we had to invent that ourselves based on what we learned about each composer. Our work was clearly a project, a solo project at that – however, it required the cooperation of the class to perform.

In my book, *Arts Integration*, I write more extensively about theories of learning. I'm most fascinated by Jean Piaget and his studies of how children learn. Jean Piaget (1963) is known for constructivist theory and developmental stages, and he writes that "intelligence is an adaptation.... Life is a continuous creation of increasingly complex forms and a progressive balancing of these forms with the environment" (p. 3). He describes intelligence as an ongoing construction of knowledge, the process being one of continual adaptation. In a somewhat parallel discussion, Lev Vygotsky (1971) defines art in a similar manner. He writes, "from a social viewpoint, art is a complex process of balancing the environment" (p. 294). One wonders what kind of conversation Piaget and Vygotsky might have concerning the relationship between intelligence, art, and environment.

I am particularly drawn to Piaget's characterization of the process of learning in the context of Project-based learning because he emphasizes an evolving thought process rather than a static outcome. In other words, learning by "doing" or through some sort of project would be at the core of what Piaget would consider learning versus memorizing facts would not constitute learning from Piaget's point of view! To learn, as his student Constance Ka-mii coined the phrase, is to invent. We can think of Project-based learning as a method that engages students in a process with a future rather than the acquisition of a knowledge base as a matter of fact. Although intellectual development is often gauged in terms of answers reported on a test or the retelling of a historical event, these devices leave little room for assessing creative and reflective thinking. Piaget also stresses, along with Vygotsky, that the work is an effort toward balancing, and the balancing is related to one's environment.

In utilizing the arts integration and Project-based learning, my goal is to engage students in thoughtful inquiry and reflective questioning. To that end, both music and the use of music as an art form can provide a method that enables each student to represent and translate ideas into something new. While they work through their understandings – perhaps in an effort to find balance – I want students to be constantly aware and able to perceive aspects of their world from many perspectives. I want them to accept risks in their thinking and be willing to live with confusion. Finally, I want them to accept what they have learned as incomplete. After all, in both teaching and learning, there is always somewhere else to go with one's ideas. Like Piaget, I believe that intellectual development is a nonending, continuous, and life-long process.

Though Piaget, and the work of his students, has held up over time, I've also been drawn to understanding the challenges and limitations of Project-based learning, or learning from the future. There probably is nothing Project-based that will ultimately take over shredding on your instrument or memorizing the circle of fifths. That being said, there are creative ways to learn to practice, and nearly everything that requires discipline.

Concluding Thoughts

C. Otto Scharmer (2016) has written extensively about "leading from the fu-ture as it emerges" and presents workshops including music examples and social theater work. From Piaget to Scharmer, we have that "swing" that makes learning come alive for students and places students in the center of the learning process. Teaching, learning and Project-based learning in the music Higher Education classroom require a mindful shift in teaching. This shift hands over the possibility of learning to the students, with the teacher or professor as the guide or coach. In some manner, the handing over of learning to students will also require an open mind, heart, and open will. This kind of learning will disrupt what students may be used to or expect. However, such disruptions will often result in opening the door toward thoughtful action and reflection.

Bibliography

Goldberg, Merryl Ruth. *Arts Integration: Teaching Subject Matter Through the Arts in Multicultural Settings*. New York: Routledge, 2017.

Hawkins, David. *The Informed Vision: Essays on Learning and Human Nature*. New York: Algora, 2002.

Piaget, Jean. *The Origins of Intelligence in Children/Jean Piaget*. Transl. by Margaret Cook. New York: W. W. Norton & Company, 1963.

Scharmer, C. Otto. *Theory U: Leading from the Future as it Emerges: The Social Technology of Presencing*. San Francisco, CA: Berrett-Koehler, 2016.

Vygotskij, Lev Semenovič. *The Psychology of Art* (Psychologija iskusstva, engl.) Lev Semenovich Vygotsky. Cambridge, MA: MIT Press, 1971. Also check out this website for arts advocacy tools and tons of research: www.csusm.edu/artopp/.

Part I
Music History and Appreciation

3
Open Classrooms, Problem-Based Learning, and Adjunct Instructors

JOHN THOMERSON

John Thomerson equates Problem-based Learning with the open classroom philosophy of music educator Randall Allsup and situates his PBL application within that larger framework. From there, John examines challenges in implementation in terms of shifting classroom roles and asynchronicity in his Music Appreciation course. He then rethinks his PBL as a pedagogy of searching for answers rather than achieving them, something which could achieve more than educated students, but curious lifelong learners.

~

Framing the PBL

In this chapter, I suggest that Problem-based Learning (PBL) offers one method for opening our classrooms and our teaching. I argue that PBL aligns with Randall Allsup's philosophy of open classrooms, and I present and critique a model PBL activity I deployed to open my teaching. I focus on the particular challenges adjunct instructors face when implementing this approach. Contingent faculty face unique difficulties to leading pedagogical reforms, and targeting this audience, the dominant force in college and university teaching, spotlights the potential benefits and systemic barriers to implementing open, PBL-influenced music classrooms. I conclude by suggesting ways the core ideas of open instruction and PBL can apply to other instructional settings.

Randall Allsup's *Remixing the Classroom* makes a passionate argument for "opening" our music instruction to address the challenges facing contemporary American education, including both structural elements (globalization, the nature of late capitalism, and the effects of privilege and systemic inequality) and institutional ones (shrinking arts and humanities budgets in K-12 and higher education as well as the demands of the Global

Educational Reform Movement, which attempts to create cost-effective, hierarchical, measurement-driven schools by focusing on assessment, efficiency, standardization, productivity, and meritocracy). Allsup also articulates a number of discipline-specific issues including the tension inherent in teaching a fixed and largely cultivated repertoire to students whose musical backgrounds and interests often favor vernacular music and our dominant philosophical paradigm and a Master-apprentice teaching model propagated through a culture of praxial instruction. To confront these overlapping challenges, Allsup argues that we must find "alternative ways to address university music-teacher education and the practice of teaching music" (Allsup, xi).

PBL offers instructors one way to open our practice, focusing less on teaching a tradition (any tradition) and more on creating encounters that maximize the possibilities inherent in a "teacher's unrepeatable moment in time" and place with her students. Allsup emphasizes the unknowable, the unfinished, and the unpredictable, encouraging us to listen to new frequencies, particularly from voices customarily dispossessed from the conventional methods and topics of music education. Listening to such voices requires openness as an orientation toward human relationships, which manifests in our teaching through increasing flexibility, a shift in focus to exploration and human growth, and concern with "events and relationships" that manifest as "irreducible, locally governed, and unfinished," as well as often without a "general consensus about what is good and what is bad" (Allsup, ix–xii). PBL's focus on open-ended, real-world problems provides students with a space for exploring those relationships.

It is worth addressing a potential objection to my use of "PBL" throughout this chapter: some authors, including John Savery, argue that PBL "must be the pedagogical base in the curriculum and not part of a didactic curriculum" (Savery, 14). This presents a problem for music educators because no existing studies – including Hon-Lun Yang's article in the *Journal of Music History Pedagogy* or those in this volume, which constitute the first substantial application of PBL to collegiate music instruction – apply PBL to an entire curriculum. Given the dearth of research on this modality and music studies, I argue that implementing a PBL-influenced approach in a variety of collegiate music courses is a necessary starting point for ascertaining the strengths and weaknesses of this approach in our discipline and gathering the data necessary for supporting curricular reform.

Background and Course Information

I implemented PBL during the spring of 2016 in Music History in Western Civilization II, the second portion of a required two-semester sequence for sophomore music majors. Scheduling issues and enrollment vagaries resulted in two uneven sections of 27 and 63 students, the majority of whom were music education majors. I divided the students in groups based on instrument type or voice part, which necessitated combining students from multiple sections into one section because several instrumentalists in the smaller class lacked partners.

My motivation to investigate and implement PBL grew out of a desire to implement an experiential learning strategy and through frustration stemming from my experiences as an adjunct. Like many contingent faculty, the majority of my teaching involves lower-level "service courses" intended for students who are interested in the subject insofar as they are less interested in the other courses that fulfill the same graduation requirement. Because much of the current rhetoric around college education in the United States focuses on its practical, tangible, market-oriented outcome, engaging these students – even in classes intended for majors – can be a challenge, and many students in music history survey courses consider the subject of little relevance to their performing, learning, and teaching.

I was also drawn to both Allsup's work and PBL because of their basis in learner-centered teaching. Maryellen Weimer's *Learner-Centered Teaching: Five Key Changes to Practice* describes a reformulation away from traditional instructor-centered pedagogy that involves several foundational shifts in classroom power, the role of teachers and of students, the function of content, and in the process and purpose of evaluation. For Allsup, the traditional structures of the classroom are upended when teachers cast off the Master's mantle and make a "concerted and conscious" effort to share "power and control" (Allsup, 12). PBL instruction likewise necessitates a shift in power away from a conventional (and authoritarian) "sage on the stage" style of professor-centric teaching and towards increased agency and responsibility for students. One of PBL's chief elements requires instructors to abandon their customary role as lecturers. Instead, they create or select "ill-structured problems" (Savery, 12). These "messy, real-world problems" are "complex," lack "a single correct answer," and involve integrating knowledge from different domains (Hmelo-Silver, 235; Savery, 12; Torp and Sage, 15).

I hoped that opening my teaching practice through PBL's open-ended questioning would engage students in the act of music history, with musicology as a verb. I wanted my students to develop the higher-order thinking skills required to fulfill our course's objective to "describe the challenges and opportunities involved in writing music history," and I presented them with a question that would demonstrate a practical application of the term's content: How would you teach the history of your instrument or voice type? As Hon-Lun Yang's research found, designing an appropriate question is challenging. These problems must be "engaging and motivating," be anchored in the "real world," have multiple potential solutions, provide "stimulus for collaborative enquiry, and contribute toward learning outcomes." She admits that even with her own work, "there is no doubt that the chosen problems need to be revisited and refined if PBL is to be continued," a conclusion I extend to my work (Yang, 330).

Implementing the PBL

Answering this question involves a shift in power and classroom roles. During PBL, instructors function as tutors guiding (but not micromanaging) the learning process and encouraging self-reflection and metacognition. In their role as tutors, faculty "support the process" and "expect learners to make their thinking clear," without providing "information related to the problem," a research task that remains the learners' responsibility (Savery, 12–14, 16). As Savery's description suggests, student roles also shift during this process as students increase their personal responsibility for their learning, a noteworthy departure from Paulo Freire's "banking theory" of education, a mental model that many student share. A key component of this shift involves students' awareness of their existing knowledge. Students have both the agency and responsibility to fill in gaps in their understanding through self-directed research, the point of which "is for individuals to collect information that will inform the group's decision-making process in relation to the problem" (Savery, 13–14). Through their work with an in-class background knowledge prompt, my students recalled and organized their existing knowledge on the subject. During class, students completed a think-pair-share with five questions: "What do you know that you could use to solve this problem?"; "What do you need to know that you could use to solve this problem?"; "Where could you learn this?"; "How could you organize this information?"; and "What are potential ways of presenting this information?" While they had a general sense of the history of their applied instrument or voice type, each student articulated a need for further research regarding specific details as well as a method for organizing this information.

From their work with this prompt, students developed plans for investigating what they did not know and more importantly, understood that the problem involved answering two different yet related questions: "What do we teach?" and "How do we teach it?" Despite beginning their work in class, some students did not realize the work they did with this prompt offered a foundation for beginning their research. As one of my music education colleagues recommended, it proved important that I remind students they had started the project already in class and reassure them that their discomfort was a natural part of the learning process. During the subsequent class meeting, I provided a skeletal framework for their work over the next three weeks: "explore pre-existing knowledge, identify areas where more information is needed, critically research this information and integrate it into existing knowledge, build on this information to identify different ways of solving this problem, and agree on and deliver one solution."

Another challenge that arose from creating groups of students in different sections was that their work was done asynchronously out of class. Not only were students responsible for finding answers to their questions (rather than relying on the instructor to tell them information), they also had to share and synthesize those answers with their group members. Savery considers such collaboration an "essential" component of PBL work. Team members obtain solutions by balancing individual contributions within a collective vision, sharing what they "learned and how that information might impact" their development of solutions to the problem (Savery, 13–14). This collaboration proved hard to spark; several students wanted or needed a response from group members in another section but were reluctant to assume responsibility for communicating with them. Many students hoped leadership would materialize in their groups but were unwilling or unable to accept such a role themselves. I believe this passivity highlights the importance of a curricular approach to PBL: students would be familiar with the expectations of such work if it was used as the basis for their instruction. As facilitator one of my key tasks was communicating the importance of collaboration, and I found that asking in-class self-reflection questions encouraged students to conceive of themselves as contributors to their group. We spent a portion of one class meeting metacognating on the collaborative process, with students reflecting on the biggest contribution they could make to their group's progress this week, what they needed from their group members, and (most importantly) what actions they would take based on this self-reflection.

Shifts in power structures and classroom roles necessitate similar changes in the use of content and the purposes of learning as well as the way teachers assess this learning. Allsup's focus on openness and what he calls "third meanings" suggests that the purpose of learning is not a tangible product or definitively assessable student outcome ("play a C major scale at 120 beats per minute" or "explain the importance of the Heiligenstadt Testament") but rather the process of searching itself. He argues we should not conceive of music instruction as the transmission of a set of closed techniques and forms to students but rather as a space "in which people can connect with others across difference and ability in an ongoing and unfinished way." Content in such instances consists not of a technique or set repertory to be mastered but the ideas that can create these spaces (Allsup, 106). Similarly, the content in PBL is not merely the objective data and subjective interpretations that constitute a discipline's knowledge but the ways of conceiving of problems, conducting research, and approaching solutions that typify disciplinary thinking. The purpose of PBL is not only to help students learn more about a particular subject but also to understand the topic's complexities. To answer their question, my students deepened their historical knowledge and faced problems that musicologists encounter, including evaluating and synthesizing information from a variety of primary and secondary sources, resolving any contradictions their research uncovered, and tailoring research findings for specific audiences. They also began to recognize that history is not a closed book, that historians disagree on or remain uncertain of answers to sometimes even basic questions, and that the choices historians make can have a significant effect on how individuals are remembered (or forgotten). While these concepts often provide a subtext to conventional instructor-centered lectures, opening a classroom through PBL makes these issues explicit topics of study.

Assessment

During our final class meeting, my students evaluated their contributions and those of their group members to their final projects and responded to other prompts designed to encourage metacognition. They also synthesized their new understanding of musicology through a closing analysis that included a presentation of their group's solution and several writing assignments. Savery considers the reflective components of these self and peer assessments some of the most important elements of PBL (Savery, 14). These prompts built on work we had done each week during our process, when students answered questions that related their projects to course content. These questions were factual (connecting specific information to broader themes) as well as interpretive (dealing with issues of representation and value judgement in historical narratives). During our final session, my students articulated and justified the criteria they had used to include and exclude certain epochs, styles, and artists from their histories. We had a vigorous concluding debate that dealt with issues of representation: who's included, who's excluded, and why; how people and ideas are discussed, and what relationships are made between them; and what value judgements (implicit or explicit) are made, what criteria are used to make them, and why these judgements are made. Students connected their work to these issues of representation and historiography, addressing the choices they made as well as those they did not make. This work encouraged a perspective shift, as students stepped back from the detail-oriented nature of writing their history to construct a broader understanding of how their work fit into our semester's narrative.

While several groups submitted work that suggested limited engagement with the question or little effort tailoring their history for a specific audience, most groups presented interesting results, including topics or repertory that are traditionally absent from Western music survey courses. One section of percussionists wrote a specialist history that embraced Western and "World" drumming traditions. Their history moved from African instruments like the *gyil* and *balafon* to Gamelan ensembles to orchestral and band mallet percussion, spotlighting differences and similarities in construction, tuning, performance technique, and social function. A section of altos conducted ethnographic interviews to illustrate differences in vocal pedagogy between

American and Chinese music schools. Several saxophonists embraced the historiographical challenge inherent in teaching the history of a relatively new instrument. They weighed the advantages and disadvantages of several approaches: How does the saxophone's history change if we focus on famous individuals as opposed to schools of playing? What about writing a material history of the instrument? What do we include of the sax's use in a broad range of styles? What about writing a history of the instrument by its function in various ensembles? Their final project combined elements from all these approaches, which they enriched with materials from Reed Library's Rascher Archive.

I was especially interested in how groups of different students presented the same instrument or voice type. One group of sopranos took a "big picture" narrative approach, describing for a general audience how their voice part's function changed from Ancient Greece to the present; another section focused on performers to categorize different classifications of the soprano voice. A group of pianists relied on their experiences physically playing the instrument to offer insight into the impact of a composer's style and changes in instrument design across a 100-year period. Their approach lent itself to both specialist and generalist audiences, as did the lecture-demonstration format of their colleagues' presentation.

Despite this variety, much of my students' work was similar to presentations I gave in class, affirming the necessity of providing a variety of models to shape student behavior and suggesting that PBL should be designed backward into an existing course to best demonstrate the process of musicology rather than the products of music history. Such a design challenges contingent instructors. Because adjuncts often have limited input into a course's learning objectives as well as marginal control over a course's design, I recommend contingent faculty consider issues of design and assessment before choosing to integrate PBL into their pedagogy. Notwithstanding these potential problems, the advantages to this approach were apparent in the myriad ways my students' narratives deemphasized canonical composers and repertory. They attended to "new frequencies" by focusing on composers, performers, and instruments that were marginal to our course's primary narrative, underscoring the shift in emphasis that can occur as performers began writing music history. Their work exemplified the idea that understanding "histories" in the plural captures the diversity bubbling under the surface of our archetypically closed form as well as the fragility of conventional historical narratives when they are exposed to new perspectives.

This idea led to interesting conversations in our concluding discussion, which touched on historiography, the history of musicology, and recent shifts in what the field values and how it justifies these judgements. These discussions highlighted the relationships between the students' PBL work and the material we addressed in class, while also re-centering musicology as an active process continually under revision, a model that challenged their notions of music history as a static body of knowledge. The idea that musicology offers a way of thinking about music – just like theory, analysis, and performance – was a fundamental and powerful concept underlying our course. From our first meeting, I worked to challenge my students' existing ideas of history, moving from an understanding of music history as a static, complete, objective, work-based body of knowledge to a dynamic, ongoing, subjective, context-specific way of understanding texts and performances. Focusing on these fundamental and powerful concepts enriched my students' PBL work and gave them a new framework through which to construct knowledge during this project (Nosich, 101–5).

Reflections on the PBL

Despite its positive impact on student learning, PBL poses challenges that are exacerbated by the limitations confronted by contingent faculty. Adjuncts face barriers to developing and refining their implementation of PBL across semesters because teaching assignments can shift or be canceled with little notice, and they are unable to incorporate PBL into a larger curriculum because such decisions are usually made without substantive input from adjunct faculty. Adjuncts can also struggle to secure the student investment in PBL that established faculty could more readily evoke and to disrupt prevailing expectations created by tenured faculty. In my case, the course was a graduation requirement that, by practice, involved limited work for students overwrought by other curricular pressures. Given my short tenure at the institution, I had little opportunity to alter these expectations, and getting students to work out of class was an unanticipated challenge. Implementing PBL on a semester-long basis would have helped my students transition from closed to open classrooms and move beyond their natural discomfort with a new learning modality (further evidence supporting the idea that PBL works best as a curricular approach and not a one-off experiment). I would also offer increased space for student questions (both in and out of class) to benefit students who thought any time in class not spent on lectures was wasted. Such scaffolding might have minimized issues related to student motivation. Several of my students remarked that they saw this work as another academic exercise divorced from reality, a claim which would be avoided through a substantive service learning component that would engage student musicians with their communities. Future iterations of my PBL will have students move beyond the initial question to include selecting an audience, presenting their work, and refining their history based on this experience. This work poses additional challenges, however, as adjuncts can be unaware of university and community resources and can struggle to secure the necessary support from department and university administration (I was fortunate: my work was supported at both the institutional and system levels, but this is not always the case for adjuncts using new pedagogical approaches).

Another issue facing adjunct instructors involves the time and funding available for frequent assessment, an issue that is complicated by PBL's open-ended nature. I avoided using a rubric because there were multiple correct solutions to the problem and because I considered a rubric's prescriptive qualities contrary to the spirit of PBL's spirit of free inquiry. Given the large number of students I had, limited support for extensive feedback, and the newness of PBL work in this setting, I opted to grade each project pass/fail. This was a mistake because the assessment criteria did not specify markers of quality and resulted in some groups doing minimal work. More important, however, was my missed opportunity to have students engage critically with a variety of sources and use these to articulate the qualities of good historical writing and the problems historians must solve when writing for different audiences. In the future, I would work with students to guide their creation of a rubric that exemplifies these traits, further opening the classroom to give them a voice in how they will be assessed. I would also change my grading to reflect the process nature of PBL by incorporating low-stakes informal assessments in several stages.

Perhaps the most significant challenge adjuncts will encounter – one that manifested in a number of ways during this project – is student resistance. This can be an expected result of a shift towards learner-centered teaching, and I recognize that several decisions I made during the project exacerbated these difficulties. One particular issue was my insistence on hewing close to the spirit of PBL in terms of providing open-ended responses to questions, which several students found frustrating. When evaluating the work-to-knowledge benefits of their PBL experience and sharing their recommendations for continued exploration of this learning modality, some students were adamant that the project took away from class time or that any project should have clear guidelines. They argued they "came to class to learn" (equating lecturing with learning) and did not want to change that. I was unprepared for this line of criticism particularly given what I had perceived as the success of my introduction to PBL. I opened our work by introducing my students to our problem and to how PBL differed from conventional pedagogical approaches. I increased investment at the beginning of this work by framing PBL as a positive response to problems posed by state-standardized testing (New York's dreaded Regents Exams) and by providing background on PBL as a learning modality. By the end of our class session, students demonstrated an understanding of what PBL involved for them as learners. The general tenor of responses was positive, with several students sharing their excitement for the practical applicability of the work or their eagerness for the type of learning they had expected at the college level. It is worth noting that the majority of students praised PBL's self-directed components, which they believed encouraged them to take agency in their learning, and they reacted positively towards the idea of using PBL in the future. Despite this, given the precarious status of contingent faculty, student resistance could make the difference between contract renewal and unemployment.

Overall, adjunct instructors should be aware that their PBL work will involve a considerable investment of time especially during the first iteration. Both design elements and issues of student resistance come to the fore, and meaningful feedback might fall beyond the scope of practice of part-time faculty. I admit that the realities of life as an adjunct impacted my PBL design, sometimes shifting my primary concerns from the pedagogic to the logistic. Given the realities of contingent faculty labor, the expanded workload created by implementing new teaching strategies, and the increased potential for negative student responses, I caution adjunct instructors against implementing PBL, regardless of its efficacy or its potential impact on student learning, without substantive prior consideration of these issues and discussions with partners/spouses, faculty, administration, and other stakeholders.

Despite these reservations, I can claim unequivocally that my practice has benefited from Allsup's ideas on open music instruction and the core ideas of PBL. While adjuncts lack the power to institute the changes required for a curricular use of PBL, I believe the approach holds promise for music instruction. While music offers a quintessential example of experiential learning, a musical apprentice's learning is typically top-down and highly controlled by Masters; students learn to replicate, but not create, and they have little say in either the process or product of their instruction. What would happen if faculty opened their teaching? What if students had greater responsibility for their learning, and this learning was done not in an artificial academic setting but one that recreated the challenges and stresses faced by working musicians? Private instruction offers one starting point. While groups are required for "true" PBL, I have used its principles to open my guitar lessons to good effect. This is an inefficient process by conventional metrics – it takes students longer to solve problems than it would for me to fix them – but is one that creates opportunities for my students develop practical, real-world skills that can benefit them in a range of scenarios. A second example is inspired by a student comment that "PBL involved an ensemble approach" to learning: what if ensemble rehearsals were run on disaggregated principles, like those modeled by the Orpheus Chamber Ensemble? While a process of collective rehearsal would be messier without an authoritative leader, students would learn and practice a host of higher-level thinking and collaboration skills that are absent in the rote responses to typical rehearsal instruction. One final example: open classrooms and PBL have significant potential in under-resourced classrooms. Growing up in adverse environments alters brain chemistry, manifesting in a student's heightened "fight or flight" impulses, which in turn hampers student learning and exacerbates the other problems created by growing up in poverty.

Researchers have found that "soft" or noncognitive skills like determination, grit, and perseverance are imperative for the success of these students – skills that, it should go without saying, are foundational elements of any music instruction. PBL offers an unconventional way of engaging these learners as well as developing noncognitive skills; while issues of student resistance and lack of initial investment in this student population can be heightened, I have found engagement and retention improve when open principles are applied.

Open and PBL-style teaching strategies promote active, cooperative learning experiences that allow students to create and integrate information in a deep way. These approaches destabilize our classrooms: they are unpredictable, sometimes inefficient, and often frightening, but they also test our musicianship, forge genuine connections with our students, and model a democratic exploration of our materials and roles and musics. PBL has the potential to open our pedagogy, to create spaces of inclusion where students are participants in traditions instead of merely observers, trying and failing and experiencing and musicking. While this opening process tests our conventional methods – and presents adjuncts with several serious issues to consider before adopting such approaches – I second Allsup's urging to "move beyond the comfortable" and seek the "pleasure and peril of renewal" in our teaching (Allsup, x and 141).

Acknowledgments

I am grateful for the support I received throughout my research from Dr. Melvin Unger, director of Fredonia's School of Music, from musicology faculty Michael Markham and James Davis, and from Dawn Eckenrode at Fredonia's Professional Development Center.

Bibliography

Allsup, Randall Everett. *Remixing the Classroom: Toward an Open Philosophy of Music Education*. Bloomington and Indianapolis, IN: Indianapolis University Press, 2016.

Burkholder, J. Peter. "The Value of a Music History Survey." *Journal of Music History Pedagogy* 5 (2015): 57–63.

Freire, Paulo. "The 'Banking' Concept of Education." In *Ways of Reading*, edited by David Bartholomae and Anthony Petrosky, 242–54. Boston, MA: Bedford-St. Martin's, 2008.

Gibson, Don. "The Curricular Standards of NASM and Their Impact on Local Decision Making." *Journal of Music History Pedagogy* 5 (2015): 73–76.

Hmelo-Silver, Cindy E. "Problem-Based Learning: What and How Do Students Learn?" *Educational Psychology Review* 16 (2004): 235–66.

Jonassen, David H. and Woei Hung. "Problem-Based Learning." In *Encyclopedia of the Sciences of Learning*, edited by Norbert M. Seel, 2687–90. New York: Springer, 2012.

Lowe, Melanie. "Rethinking the Undergraduate Music History Sequence in the Information Age." *Journal of Music History Pedagogy* 5 (2015): 65–71.

Moore, Robin D., ed. *College Music Curricula for a New Century*. New York: Oxford University Press, 2017.

Nosich, Gerald. *Learning to Think Things Through: A Guide to Critical Thinking Across the Curriculum*. Upper Saddle River, NJ: Prentice Hall, 2011.

Roust, Colin. "The End of the Undergraduate Music History Sequence?" *Journal of Music History Pedagogy* 5 (2015): 49–51.

Savery, John R. "Overview of Problem-Based Learning: Definitions and Distinctions." *Interdisciplinary Journal of Problem-Based Learning* 1 (2006): 9–20.

Seaton, Douglass. "Reconsidering Undergraduate Music History: Some Introductory Thoughts." *Journal of Music History Pedagogy* 5 (2015): 53–56.

Tai, Gillian Xiao-Lian and May Chan Yuen, "Authentic Assessment Strategies in Problem Based Learning." In *ICT: Providing Choices for Learners and Learning—Proceedings ascilite Singapore* 2007, 983–93. Accessed August 24, 2016. www.ascilite.org/conferences/singapore07/procs/.

Tough, Paul. *Helping Children Succeed: What Works and Why.* Boston, MA: Houghton Mifflin, 2016.

Torp, Linda and Sara Sage. *Problems as Possibilities: Problem-Based Learning for K–16 Education.* Alexandria, VA: Association for Supervision and Curriculum Development, 2002.

Walker, Andrew, Heather Leary, Cindy Hmelo-Silver, and Peggy A. Ertmer, eds. *Essential Readings in Problem-Based Learning: Exploring and Extending the Legacy of Howard S. Barrows.* West Lafayette, IN: Purdue University Press, 2015.

Walsh, Allyn. *The Tutor in PBL: A Novice's Guide.* Hamilton, ON: McMaster University, 2005.

Weimer, Maryellen. Learner-Centered Teaching: Five Key Changes to Practice. San Francisco, CA: Jossey-Bass, 2002.

Woods, Donald R. "Preparing for PBL." Third edition, 2006. Accessed September 27, 2016. www.chemeng.mcmaster.ca/sites/default/files/media/Woods-Preparing-for-PBL.pdf.

Yang, Hon-Lun. "Teaching Music History at Hong Kong Baptist University: Problem-Based Learning and Outcome-Based Teaching and Learning." *Journal of Music History Pedagogy* 4 (2014): 329–32.

4
Problem-Based Learning in the Music Appreciation Course

MARGARET LEENHOUTS

> *Margaret's chapter illustrates one of the classic examples of Problem-based Learning – a Music Appreciation course in which students create an orchestra season for a particular audience. The chapter situates the PBL within a general population college classroom, in which students are not only nonmusic majors, but many have never witnessed a live concert. This problem asks students to work "tangibly with the material and their own aesthetic judgements in a realistic and fun manner," not only overcoming their lack of concert-going experience but also requiring them to think through all of the issues and difficulties inherent in creating a publicly consumed series of community value by applying the content learned throughout the semester and then some.*

~

Background

MUS 210, the course I teach at The College at Brockport, is a Music Appreciation course with a twist; the course is traditionally taught by a member of a professional orchestra and includes regular demonstrations and lectures by members of the Rochester Philharmonic Orchestra and other local performing artists. As a part of the exurban area of Rochester, New York, Brockport – a small village to the west of the city – is well situated for this mission. The nearby Eastman School of Music, one of the major conservatories in the United States, has peppered the region with many fine musicians and artists from a great variety of styles and genres. For this class, I have brought in guests that work in small groups and combos, allowing the students to see musicians at work in a realistic setting.

In order to accommodate the Philharmonic members' schedule, the class is taught on Monday evenings from 6:30 to 9:15, a time when the orchestra rarely rehearses or gives concerts. The textbook for the course is *In Performance* by

Wayne Bailey (2015), which approaches the topic through typical venues: concert hall, theater and film, church, and recital hall. This allows students to include the idea of function in their thinking about the music. Is the music written primarily to entertain, inspire, accompany a large social gathering, or some combination of all these?

In our discussion of the music of the concert hall, for example, students learn about the form, aesthetics, and conventions of major concert genres including the concerto, symphony, suite, and symphonic poem along with a discussion of the ways these genres have changed over time. We listen to several examples of each genre allowing the class to delve into the details of the music and its creator. For instance, exploring the symphony entails comparing movements of the works of Haydn, Beethoven, Brahms, Berlioz, Dvorak, and Larsen; examining how each work is not only a unique expression of its creator but also representative of its cultural and temporal milieu.

Students generally take the course in order to fulfill their General Education requirements. The College requires at least two courses in the fine arts so that students will be able to "demonstrate an understanding of at least one principal form of artistic expression and the creative process inherent therein." Music appreciation is concerned principally with the first of these outcomes – an understanding of the form of music. The course may also be taken, however, as a part of the requirements of the music minor; thus, the musical skills, experiences, and interests of the students vary widely.

Enrollment in the course fluctuates and is always smaller in the spring than in the fall when most students attempt to satisfy their General Education requirements. It is also typical in this large public university to lose about 20% of the students during the course of the semester. Most drop out in the first two weeks of the semester, but it is common to lose three or four students mid-semester as work schedules and grades take a toll on academic lives. In the spring of 2017, Music Appreciation began with 20 students and ended with 17, including one attendee who audited the course and did not participate in the project.

Brockport defines clearly the Student Learning Outcomes (SLOs) for its General Education courses. For a Fine Arts course emphasizing knowledge of the form of an art, they are the following:

1. *Demonstrate knowledge of music from a historical and cultural perspective*
   - Identify specific works or styles of music produced by artists in different periods or cultures
   - Articulate (through any number of means) the role of music and its impact on society/culture

- Identify connections between music and its historical and/or cultural contexts
2. *Apply critical thinking skills to the discipline of music*
    - Analyze and evaluate information, propositions, and statements regarding music
    - Form a process of reflection, examine the offered evidence, and form judgements about facts
    - Articulate the pros and cons of a particular music-based problem
3. *Ability to locate music and information about music from a variety of sources*
    - Recognize and obtain key ideas, events, dates, places, people, and information from both digital and non-digital sources
    - Describe and understand information, and translate information into a new setting
    - Interpret or contrast sets of information, and predict implications.
4. *Ability to make connections between music and the community at large*
    - Identify social systems, ideologies, and cultures in which music functions
    - Understand music's functions and performance practices in relation to differing cultural behaviors, ethnic backgrounds, religions, sexual orientations, disabilities, and other diversity factors in a manner that recognizes, affirms, and values the worth of individuals, communities, and families and protects and preserves the dignity of each
    - Discuss attitudes, skills, and knowledge through which individuals and systems respond respectfully, empathically, and effectively to people who are different.

In addition to the PBL project, students are asked to attend three concerts or class presentations and write a review for each, as well as take weekly quizzes, a midterm, and a final exam.

The Project

I was excited about the prospect of designing a new project that would both address the College's SLOs and might ameliorate some of the inherent difficulties in the course. Because most students arrive with little or no knowledge of music history, theory, or performance, the course heavily emphasizes information. Students are faced with a block of 2 hours and 45 minutes of new music and new information each week. Having attended several rock concerts during my children's 'tween years, I am sympathetic to the difficulty of listening to multiple hours of new music in one sitting.

In addition, music, by its nature, is abstract, ephemeral, and deeply personal. The meaning and emotions conveyed are completely individual, and it can be uncomfortable for both students and professor to lack a "right" answer. I have often found it difficult to elicit meaningful discussions of the music's effect in class. Therefore, I wanted an assignment that would give students a chance to work tangibly with the material and their own aesthetic judgements in a realistic and fun manner. I also wanted to increase the social cohesion of the group in order to increase the involvement and participation of the entire class.

I developed the following project to be completed over the course of the semester. Students were presented with the following rubrics at the initial class meeting.

Create an Orchestra Season Problem-based Learning (20% of Grade)

Form groups of 4 or 5 members. Your group is the board of a musical arts organization in a small city. You will put together a season of 4 concerts with broad appeal to the community.

a) At least one piece from each historical era must be in the season.
b) One concert may be a recital hall offering, an educational program, or a "pops" concert.

You will develop:

1. A season brochure for your arts organization
2. A two- to three-page rationale for your programming choices

The Season Brochure must include:

1. The programs written in correct style with full information about the music, composer, time, and place of the concert, any soloists (fictional, living, historical)
2. Program notes
3. A stylish design on the cover
4. You may also want to have fun including "advertisements," biographies for any "soloists," and a roster of players

The rationale will:

1. Describe how the group arrived at its programming choices – timing, artists, music, program order – for each program
2. Explain the values and principles used to make the choices and how the choices will attract and entertain audiences.

The project addressed the above SLOs in several ways. As the students developed their programs, they had to find appropriate repertory (SLO 3), think about its aesthetic value both as a piece of music and as a part of a program (SLO 2), and consider how this music would be received by an audience (SLO 4). Writing a rationale required the students to be conscious of the values behind the decisions.

In order to produce good program notes, the students needed to investigate the historical and cultural background of their chosen repertory and present it in a coherent and meaningful way to others (SLOs 1 and 4). One class period was spent in the university library with a reference librarian investigating how to locate important sources of musical scholarship available to the students (SLO 3).

In addition to satisfying the SLOs, I envisioned that the project would permit students to:

1. Use new-found knowledge in a concrete and creative way
2. Deepen their knowledge of particular composers, pieces, and/or styles in completing the research for and in writing the program notes
3. Learn the conventions of symphonic programming – typical length, how to format a program with composer and movements included, where to include an intermission, etc.
4. Present the students with two different but useful writing tasks: the short research results included in the program notes and an argumentative paper
5. Develop an understanding of the basis of their own and other's aesthetic choices and make distinct choices of repertory with this knowledge in mind
6. Explore the enormous range of music outside of their previous experience and the confines of the textbook
7. Participate in music and artistic discussion as a social activity. Nearly all of the music in the course was originally experienced in a social setting, whereas many students today encounter music primarily individually, through their headphones
8. Be encouraged to utilize a variety of learning styles beyond my limits as an instructor
9. Foster the ability to stay on task and responsible. One-quarter of the grade depended upon submitting sections in a timely fashion and in working cooperatively with peers
10. Feel free to have fun with the material!

Table 4.1 was used as a grade sheet and gives a more detailed view of how the project was assessed.

Table 4.1 Student Submission Checklist

Submission Checklist: 10 pts		
1. Progress Report	_____/2	
2. Rough Draft	_____/2	
3. Brochure	_____/2	
4. Rationale	_____/2	
5. Review of project and peers	_____/2	
Brochure: 40 pts		
1. Contains all required portions and adheres to the parameters		_____/4
2. Programs are correctly formatted		_____/4
3. Program notes are		
a) Well researched		_____/2
b) Written with grammatically correct prose		_____/2
c) Free of typographical, spelling, and punctuation errors		_____/2
d) Correctly and adequately cited		_____/2
e) Notes illuminate and explain the music		_____/8
4. Quality of musical choices		_____/8
5. Visual appeal of the brochure		_____/8
Rationale: 20 pts		
1. Presents a logical argument for the choices		_____/10
2. Is well written		
a) Grammatically correct		_____/4
b) Free of typographical, spelling, and punctuation errors		_____/3
c) Avoids conversational language and word choices		_____/3
Peer Review: 10 pts		
1. Your effort as reviewed by your peers		_____/10
Extra Credit:		
Work shows exceptional creativity, research, and/or care		_____
Total:		_____/80

Assessment/Reflection

In order to ameliorate the typical group problem of less energetic students depending on the industrious to complete the work, I decided to give students the chance to rate each other's effort and demeanor in the group. Students therefore assessed each other on contribution, cooperation, flexibility, and participation. This strategy also addressed another major complaint students have concerning group work – that their scores will be averaged, rather than each student receiving grades for their individual contribution. In this case, the scores were tallied and averaged so that each student in a group could potentially earn a different grade.

Implementation

I envisioned the implementation of the project as fairly straightforward and simple. I introduced the project in a shortened version with a basic description and a timetable at the first class meeting. I set the following due dates in order to keep the class on track:

> March 6 – A 200- to 400-word summary of the progress of the group detailing:
> 1. Problems that have occurred and plans to fix them as well as describing the group's approach to completing the project
> 2. Difficulties and problems that your group has identified in the project itself. Tell me while I can still fix them!
>
> April 10 – Turn in a rough draft of your brochure containing:
> 1. Titles of pieces
> 2. Composer names and dates
> 3. Timing of pieces
> 4. Order of music in each program
>
> May 8 – Final copy of brochure, rationale, and peer and project review sheets

Both the summary and the rough draft were submitted by a drop box on Blackboard Learn, SUNY's web-based learning platform, and earned points simply by being punctual. The brochure, rationale, and student assessments were turned in on paper.

> Second Class: At the second meeting, I displayed and discussed a model brochure from the Rochester Philharmonic Orchestra, which normally bundles a month of programs into a booklet in order to save money. I showed the content of the programs, the existence of program notes, and the general visual appeal of a professionally produced brochure.
>
> Third Class: I distributed a brief questionnaire to aid me in sorting the students into groups. I prefer that students be socially comfortable in each group and let them have input into decisions regarding with whom they will or will not work. I had incorporated several small group discussion activities into the first three class meetings so that students could meet and get acquainted. Nevertheless, teaching a night class at a public university means having many students who

have responsibilities outside of their school work, including full- or part-time work and family obligations. In the end, I put groups together primarily on their availability outside of class. The class was divided into four small groups.

Fourth Class: Students received their group assignments and were given class time to develop an initial plan as well as to exchange contact and scheduling information.

Fifth and Sixth Classes: The first Philharmonic guest, a violist, visited the class and orchestral music in the 18th and 19th centuries was introduced and discussed.

Seventh Class: The progress summaries were due. Mid-semester provided a convenient time to prod the students to action and to discover major misconceptions in the project itself by turning in a summary of their progress. Disappointingly, most of the summaries were hurried and precursory.

Eighth to Tenth Classes: Orchestral music of the 20th century was covered as well as an introduction to opera through the Classical Era. The class also met the second Philharmonic guest, a trumpet player who brought in a jazz combo to discuss the use of jazz in the 20th century.

Eleventh Class: Students turned in a rough draft of their basic program information. This timing gave the students three weeks to research and to write the program notes, which I expected to be the bulk of the work for the project. I got a chance to check on the students' basic understanding of the programming of orchestral works and of the overall assignment. In addition, the information prepared students for the next class.

Twelfth Class: This class session was dedicated to library research and producing program notes for the brochures. A librarian presented an hour-long interactive session on music research materials available in the library and on its database, how to create a simple bibliography, and how to find additional models of program brochures. The students were then free to use the rest of the evening to research the composers and pieces from their rough-draft programs.

On the day of the final exam, students submitted the brochures and rationales and filled in an assessment for the project and a peer-evaluation and effort form.

PBL Results

Of the four constituted groups, three turned in a full and well-produced brochure. The remaining group of four students had divided the task by program, i.e. each student was responsible for the complete information of one of the programs. Only one of these students produced a program with accompanying notes; the others either submitted a partial assignment or, in one case, nothing. Although I had planned to assess the brochures as a group, I made an exception for this final group and judged the one submission on its own merits.

The full submissions were, in fact, fun to read and reasonably inventive and creative. The concerts were situated in a variety of locations with different real and fictional performers. One group decided to take an existing local performing group and constructed their programs literally by season (Figure 4.1).

Brockport *The Seasons* Concert Series

May 4th - May 8th

Fall: Thursday, May 4th - (2-6)

Winter: Friday, May 5th - (7-11)

Spring: Saturday, May 6th - (12-16)

Modern Era Lesson: Sunday, May 7th - (17-18)

Rationale: (19-21)

Sean Glennan + Andrew Stipe

Figure 4.1 Group #1 PBL final brochure

Although the students included some obvious thematic music such as Vivaldi's "Spring Concerto" to evoke their premise, other choices were subtler. Beethoven, for example, was incorporated into all of the programs except the Modern Era seminar, because of "the immense variation that can be seen through Beethoven's music….This is most likely the biggest contributor to why Beethoven was so successful in his time, and continues to be prominent in our society today" (rationale). The brochure contained full color photos of each composer to accompany the program notes.

A second group decided on producing a four-week summer festival with some high-powered sponsors. In this project, I enjoyed the daring programming and the attention to visual quality and detail. Each of the composers and pieces was given a full paragraph of information with full citations included. And how could a summer festival fail with that conducting staff! It brings new meaning to the problem of Classical music and dead white men. From the perspective of learning, I was pleased. I doubt these students would likely been aware of these historical figures before completing the project (Figure 4.2).

The final group to produce a brochure organized the four concerts by stylistic period, creating programs of Baroque, Classical, Romantic, and Modern music. In the Baroque concert, which consisted of the Monteverdi *Magnificat*, the Bach *A minor Violin Concerto*, and the Handel *Fireworks*

Figure 4.2 Group #2 PBL final brochure

Music, I found that I had been pressed into service as the violin soloist. This group was particularly adventurous in their approach; the modern concert consisted of *Appalachian Spring*, *The Rite of Spring*, and the *Piano Concerto, op.* 42 of Schoenberg. I had honestly never imagined any Expressionist being included on a student-designed concert. The program order, however, was occasionally problematic. In the Classical concert for example, the Beethoven 5th Symphony was placed ahead of intermission with only the Haydn "Surprise" Symphony after intermission. Students obviously had a good time finding their favorite pieces from each era but were not yet able to think in terms of program order.

The concept of a rationale proved difficult for every group. One group turned in five separate papers each of which resembled a reflection on the process of the completing the assignment: "When we first started our project, we were sort of in a rush because the next thing we know the rough draft was due. We all met together in the library and shot out some quick and simple ideas to get going on the assignment." Only in the end paragraph did I learn that "we wanted to have a variety of different music and composers to keep the people coming back for more each week."

Another of the groups included a paragraph under each program selection which blended the idea of program notes and a rationale. Here is the rationale for the Surprise Symphony; I have retained the misconceptions and grammatical difficulties of the original:

> The Surprise Symphony includes probably the most famous of all: a sudden fortissimo chord at the end of the otherwise piano opening theme in the variation-form second movement. The music then returns to its original quiet dynamic, as if nothing had happened. And the ensuing variations do not repeat the joke. Audience would probably like to hear the unappreciated jokes of symphonies.

Student Assessment of the Project

The students assessed the project with a questionnaire that contained the following questions:

1. What was the most difficult aspect of this project?
2. What have you learned in having solved this difficulty?
3. Did you use knowledge of other disciplines in completing this project? If so, please list.
4. Comment on the benefits and difficulties of group collaboration. Did others in your group expand your learning experience? If yes, how?
5. How has this project impacted your knowledge of music and of the nature of arts organizations in society?
6. What might improve this project?

Questions 1, 4, and 6 were designed to elicit feedback by which I could improve the project. Most students felt the most difficult aspect of the project was in communicating and finding time to work with the group. One or two mentioned feeling confused and overwhelmed by the nature of the project itself. Students would improve the project by "explaining the project in greater detail," "having more examples from past classes," and "actually putting on the project." I am unsure how I would incorporate the final idea into class time, but it is intriguing.

Questions 2, 3, 4, and 5 were designed to understand how well the students were able to achieve goals and SLOs. Since the principal difficulty that students faced was working in the group, much of the proposed learning in response centered on time management and dealing with others. One answer to question 2, for example, was simply "email is useful." Others, however, gleaned useful research and life tools when they "learned to effectively cooperate with a peer to overcome challenges" and in "Creating a rough draft (that) helped develop a guide to follow into the final project." Most students enjoyed and benefited from the session in the library with one student commenting that he had not known how many resources were available to him at the college until the library session.

Question 5 was, for me, the most important of the 6 since it dealt with the primary musical learning and gave students a chance to address the course SLOs. The responses for 5 included "I have an understanding of the phases music has gone through throughout time and how it has been represented in our everyday life" and "It takes a lot of effort and time to create concerts; I have a greater appreciation for it," as well as "It helps (sic) me understand the depth of music and what it meant to people and the composers."

Final Assessment

In many ways, this project was experimental. I had only a week to set it up, and I had no way of knowing which aspects would be most and least successful. There are, therefore, several things that I would and will do differently in the future. I had not anticipated how few of the students had experience with live music. None of them knew the normal format of a musical program, for example, with titles, movements, composers, and dates. Even the idea of creating a logical space for an intermission seemed alien to them. The presentation of the rationale as a part of the project was also problematic; the students simply did not understand what they were being asked to produce.

Some fixes to these problems might include:

1. Shortening the length of the brochure to three concerts, giving the students more time for detailed work such as proofreading
2. More clearly defining the purpose and expectations of a rationale and having them submit a short version of it with the summary mid-semester

3. Encourage students to include observations on programming and program order in the reviews of required concerts and presentations
4. Regularly discussing how the pieces in the textbook might be programmed and why
5. Including simpler program models for them to follow. The professional brochures that I furnished were overwhelming for these students
6. Additional attention could also be paid to writing and proofreading as this was a frequent difficulty for students.

Overall, the project was successful and met my envisioned goals and the SLOs of the College. It encouraged students to engage with the music and with the musical culture in a complex and creative way and gave them ample opportunity to research and write about music and musicians. In the words of one student, "I have a newfound respect for Classical music after hearing so many different types; I no longer think of it as a stale art form, but one that is forever evolving and changing."

Reference

Bailey, Wayne. *In Performance*. Oxford University Press, 2015.

5
Heightening Music Appreciation via Problem-Based Learning

RODNEY GARRISON

In the second of the chapters on Music Appreciation, Rodney takes his Problem-based Learning approach a bit further and redesigns his entire curriculum to accommodate it. While this is not required, it does yield excellent results. Using the Natalie Cole song "Take a Look" as a catalyst, students are asked to explore six different pathways toward a deeper understanding of the song, including documenting the process of exploration along the way, and reflect deeply on the impact of the process and problem through detailed self-assessments. Textual, visual, and musical analyses allowed students to find a more comprehensive context for this song and its meaning in 20th-century America.

~

Most universities in America offer some type of Music Appreciation course. Traditionally, Music Appreciation courses do not require prerequisites, are generally taken by nonmusic majors to fulfill an arts and/or humanities requirement, focus on the history and design of Western tonal music (as evinced by the large number of Music Appreciation textbooks with very similar contents), and are often the only music-centered course undergraduates take. In the spring semester of 2016 at State University of New York (SUNY) Fredonia's School of Music, I was again assigned to teach this institutionalized model of Music Appreciation for nonmajors. After learning about the potential benefits of Problem-based Learning (PBL) during the previous semester, I decided to implement this new teaching approach in a section of Music Appreciation. With little time or, as it turned out, need to dramatically alter the entire course, I chose to implement a PBL unit at the beginning of the semester in order to address a perceived, systemic problem within the institutionalized model. The PBL unit was also designed to seamlessly lead into the traditional goals of studying the history and design of Western tonal music from the Renaissance through Romanticism.

My impetus for learning about and ultimately applying PBL in Music Appreciation was to overcome what I perceived to be a fundamental deficiency in traditional and online Music Appreciation texts: students are not taught what the word "appreciation" means in a particularly in-depth and nuanced way, and this deficiency ensures that many will not learn how to curate a deeper and more meaningful appreciation of music. Music Appreciation texts tend to focus on a broad span of music history, teaching students to recognize characteristic musical ideas, both conceptually and aurally. In order to avoid creating texts equivalent to inactive museum displays in sterile, glass cases, authors typically include listening charts and guides. However, very little content available to students is truly interactive or exploratory. Texts need teachers to create interaction and genuine exploration – the kind of exploration that is not within the text's control or even purview.

My primary motivation in redesigning the Music Appreciation curriculum to include PBL was the realization that it is my responsibility to provide students with what may be a final opportunity to learn about and experience a deeper understanding of music appreciation. I deliberately included a PBL unit designed to interactively guide students to and through resources that collectively define "appreciation," "music appreciation," and "music research." Students experienced multiple cycles of discovery, lecture, interaction, research, and exploration during the unit's class meetings and assessments. General goals of Music Appreciation courses, such as reading and listening comprehension, as well as skills in English composition, were also addressed within the PBL unit. Despite using what I would consider a strict application of PBL for only 15%–20% of the course's duration, I found it to be effective in addressing and, to some degree, overcoming textbook and learning deficiencies.

Music Appreciation Course and PBL: Logistics and Implementation

At SUNY Fredonia in 2016, Music Appreciation was a general education credit for most students, and a required course for the Dance Bachelor of Fine Arts, Business Administration (Music Industry concentration) Bachelor of Science, and those seeking a Jazz Minor. SUNY Fredonia's learning outcome for a general education arts credit states, "Students will demonstrate: Understanding of at least one principal form of artistic expression and the creative process inherent therein." In addition to including the history and design of Western tonal music from the Renaissance through Romanticism, my Music Appreciation course also included modern Western music in at least one assignment. Students also had the option of choosing any modern Western or any non-Western music as a final research topic.

The Music Appreciation course met on a Monday, Wednesday, and Friday schedule, and each class session lasted 50 minutes. At the end of this semester-long course, four people dropped the course at various times for un-known reasons, and I submitted 43 final grades. The first unit of the five-unit course contained the PBL experience that was itself divided into two interre-lated parts: five of the six class sessions devoted to the PBL unit focused on the gradual acquisition of a deeper and more engaged understanding of music ap-preciation. One class session and two assessments – a Group/Solo Assessment and a Self-Assessment Survey that were due at the end of the unit – challenged students to put their new understandings into a less guided and more person-alized creation of an appreciation web centered on a music object. The assess-ments were formally assigned and discussed on the fourth class session. The fifth class session was dedicated to working on the Group/Solo Assessment, and during this session, students could choose to work with or without my assistance. Both PBL assessments were due on the eighth class session. Of the overall course grade, the Group/Solo Assessment was weighted as 8%, and the Self-Assessment Survey was weighted as 2%.

There were five topics devoted to the explication of Unit 1, and each topic was discussed at length in a different class session. The topics of these five sessions were designed to be interrelated and progress like a narrative, cul-minating in the two Unit 1 assessments. Each topic was formed as an in-quiry and was accompanied by two or three articles. I uploaded the articles and all other necessary course documents onto Angel, an online course management system, well in advance of their use. Students were assigned to read the articles regarding each topic before the session in which the topic was to be discussed, save the first session. The five topics of the PBL unit were:

1. Introduction to the course and PBL
2. What is fact, what is a falsehood, what is opinion, and how do they fit into objectivity and subjectivity?
3. What is appreciation, and how to we appreciate unfamiliar art? (Because my course is populated with at least a few dance majors, we looked at constructing an appreciation model of a non-Western dance.)
4. What is empirical evidence, and what do we do with it? Do emotions and empathy play a role in our observations and appreciation?
5. What is music appreciation, and how is it important to human-ity? How does self-assessment work, and can it play a role in music appreciation?

The instructions for the Group/Solo Assessment were as follows:

You are asked to construct six different paths that all lead to acquiring a deeper appreciation of the song, 'Take a Look,' as sung by Natalie Cole in 1993. You will get to know the song via the music video. You are to list six different topics you would investigate, and then, for each topic, you are to describe why you think the topic may be important to this investigation and the steps you used to investigate the topic. You must have topics regarding the music and topics regarding the text; do not dwell only on text or only on music. As of now, I am concerned with your ability to efficiently describe your creative and investigative processes, and I am not concerned with 'definitive answers' to your topics. Each topic discussion must contain at least four complete sentences, and additional sentences are welcome. Each person will turn in a copy of their answers, even if they are working with a group. After completing this assessment within a small group setting or alone – see rationale below – complete the Self-Assessment Survey on your own.

Beyond these instructions, I supplied the YouTube link to the song. For only this initial assignment, students were allowed to use any source they deemed useful. (Subsequent assignments included increasingly strict source restraints in order to gradually teach students about various source types and their usefulness.) Students created a word document that supplied their topics, reasoning for selecting each topic, and their experiences investigating each topic. Supplying bibliographic information and/or hyperlinks to sources was encouraged. Their documents could also be enriched with images, audio, and/or video, if helpful; however, enrichments could not take the place of grammatically correct prose. In total, I attempted to give only what was needed to focus observation and exploration through the lens of music appreciation, which, in my mind, created an open-ended assessment and outcome. The goals of the assessment were:

1. To use creativity to construct inquiries and investigations about the musical object
2. To formulate six different topics that pertain to the musical object and include discussion of the music and/or text
3. To reason why each topic directly relates to this musical object
4. To explain the steps of investigation taken to come to each topic and explore each topic further
5. To explain, via the self-assessment survey, how you chose to work on the Group/Solo Assessment and the experiences you had while working on it

I allowed students to complete the Group/Solo Assessment by themselves, as a pair, or in a group of three, and I provided the following reasoning:

Most of our life experiences and, resultantly, our varying appreciations of most everything are influenced by those with whom the experience is shared. As we grow older, we gain more control over with whom we share our experiences, particularly musical and other artistic experiences. Coupled with the fact that this course is not required for the majority of students, i.e., this course is self-selected for most, it seems fitting that students should have some control over their shared musical experience. This control is expressed in every student's choice to work on assignments in self-selected groups as large as three people or to work alone. Students may change groups or shift from working alone to working in a group from assignment to assignment. When it comes to groups, please keep in mind that the group, like a chain, is only as strong as its weakest link. When it comes to working alone, please understand that you may be giving up valuable insights that come from a communal experience.

PBL Outcomes and Assessment: Unit 1 Topics

Of the 43 final grades, one student did not complete the Group/Solo Assessment leaving only 42 recorded PBL experiences. It was during the initial class sessions devoted to the five discussion topics that those who dropped the course did so for unknown but probably routine reasons. This is not to say the five discussion topics leading up to the Group/Solo Assessment were banal or uneventful. Lively discussions were had that did not always end in agreement.

The second topic, "What is fact, what is opinion, and how do they fit into objectivity and subjectivity?" was the most debated topic. There were plenty of misunderstandings about the differences and connections between fact, falsehood, opinion, objectivity, and subjectivity that came to light while piecing together practical definitions of these terms in class. To test our collective and individual understanding, we put our definitions to use through the discussion of statements about wolves – statements about any topic that may or may not be accompanied by scientific data will do – and then music. First, the class heard a statement read by me, and then they, working together, quickly labeled it as best they could without the use of outside sources. Then, I read a supporting statement about the initial statement that may have been an opinion or a fact, never a falsehood. If needed, students revised their labeling of the initial statement. Other than reading statements and supporting statements, I maintained discussion orderliness and organized their collective thoughts for all to see.

The topic discussion left some students feeling unsettled because it directly confronted their prior notions of at least one of these terms, and not everyone accepted change. Of course, an understanding of these terms is crucial to being able to describe and express any object or situation with accuracy and style. Addressed in the fourth topic, "What is empirical evidence, and what do we do with it? Do emotions and empathy play a role in our observations and appreciation?" conveying empathy and appreciation to others, while seemingly understood by the conveyor, has a diminished impact on others when communicated without some intellectual rigor.

PBL Outcomes and Assessment: Unit 1 Group/Solo Assessment

In terms of music, poetry, and videography, Natalie Cole's rendition of "Take a Look" is both a timely product of the late 20th century, released the year after the deadly Los Angeles riots of 1992, and an overt reference to the American Civil Rights Movement (1954–68). Moreover, the songwriter, Clyde Otis, and arranger, Allen Toussaint, who used the pseudonym "Naomi Neville" for this song (and others), worked as professional musicians during both historic events. With many potential points of investigation from which to choose, it would be easy for students to create six paths of investigation without exhausting all possibilities, even without discussing music.

The topics students choose beyond the specified topics of music and text, and their investigative choices within topics signal a degree of willingness, comfort, and skill in developing a tight web of appreciation for the song. For example, would a student think that investigating the musical connections between the recently deceased Cole (2015) and her famous father, Nat King Cole, is a more profitable inquiry for this assessment than investigating the performance history of the song, which may or may not lead them back to Clyde Otis and the original performance by Aretha Franklin in 1967? Would a student's investigation framed in inquiry about the black-and-white videography that features people of color and glimpses of an early 1950s Oldsmobile lead them to a deeper appreciation of the song or the videography? How one frames an inquiry certainly affects and, in some cases, determines what is learned. I mentioned only the topics of music and text within the brief instructions because I hoped students would ask multiple questions within each topic. Nowhere in the instructions did I take a particular topic away from investigation. Even if a path of investigation among one or two others within a single topic does not lead to a concrete answer, the web of appreciation remains tight, as appreciation is rooted in relevant and thoughtful inquiry.

Most students and student groups submitted the required six topics for the Group/Solo Assessment, and the topics en masse were individually and best sorted into four general categories arranged by decreasing popularity and percentage of usage as compared to the entire collection of topic submissions: (1) Lyrics = 41%, (2) Videography = 25%, (3) Historical Context = 18%, and (4) Music = 16%. The following four paragraphs provide commentary on each of the four categories and their contents.

1. **Lyrics:** The most prevalent topics regarding lyrics were race, love, children, society, and religion. Topics involving lyrics appeared in everyone's list of six topics, and often more than once. As a reminder, the instructions said, "You must have topics regarding the music and topics regarding the text; do not dwell only on text or only on music." In this category, I also chose to include the handful of students that used the phrase "song's intended audience" because their explanation always centered around the meaning of text. In this category more than any other, students wrote in such a way as to find answers to their inquiries, which is something the instructions did not require. Instead of spending more time explaining their investigative process, many wrote about their textual interpretations, right or wrong as they may be. Two sample topics involving lyrics were (1) social implications of the text and (2) lyrics as a cautionary tale.

   One of the solo topics regarding lyrics was called "Imagery within the Text." This student proceeded to discuss how vividly the text conveys imagery without once mentioning the song's video. The student noted investigating the song's lyrics, with no mention of investigating imagery as a literary device. One of the group topics regarding lyrics was called "Interpreting the Song Lyrics." This group, more than most of the other participants, relied on exactly what the instructions prioritized: finding a topic to investigate, stating why the topic is worthy of investigation, and describing the investigative process without worrying about coming to conclusions about your topic/inquiry.

2. **Videography:** The students familiarized themselves with the song via the music video, but the assessment instructions did not mention whether topics only or primarily referencing the video were allowed. Excluding the video from the instructions in this way was a purposeful decision on my part, and almost all students wrote a topic that only or primarily referenced the video. Overall, there was a lack of recorded topic investigation. Of those who did record their investigations with any detail, most did not record investigating connections between the images and the lyrics. To my knowledge, there is a lack of information available to describe the videography, and this was reflected by many students who embraced an open-ended yet shallow discussion in their prose. (Sidenote: There were a few students who engaged the video's focus on the everyday lives of people of color without full engagement of the lyrics that never mention race or skin color.) Two sample topics involving videography were (1) the role of children in the music video (but oddly not the lyrics) and (2) examining the gender roles of women in the music video (and linking it to the lyrics and singer).

One of the solo topics regarding videography was called "Cinematography," and the student's only investigated sources were the video and the text. Only two direct connections from the image to the text were made: the overall positive images of the video align with the text's overall message of peace, and multiple images of children playing align with the portion of the text promoting the protection of innocent children. Music was not discussed, except to say that images in the video went well with her emotive singing. One of the group topics regarding videography was called "Singer," which does not lead one to believe the topic would be about the video. The commentary, with no investigation other than the video and the text, dwelt on the singer's position on a landing within the video. The singer's relatively high position was interpreted as a moral height above the everyday people who, in the video, are at street level. Both the solo and group topics display a lack of proper contextualization. They suggest, perhaps unwittingly, the meaning of the song begins with or is primarily determined by the video and not the lyrics.

3. **Historical Context:** Even though "historical context" is listed as a category, and this division assumes a separation from the others that may seem superficial at first, it is its own category because the word "history" or the mention of historical contexts was used as a catchall for a variety of topics. In most cases, history was not discussed in topics centered around music! More than half of the students' topics in this category inquired about Natalie Cole's life, and these inquiries were generally packed with other topics that may or may not intersect with her life. While the discussion of a single topic is brief in this assignment, many students strove to make historical points that appear to be primarily self-driven from the start or the product of shallow investigation. Two sample topics involving history were (1) Does Natalie Cole's life play a role in the song's meaning? and (2) looking at the history of race relations in the United States.

One of the solo topics regarding historical context was called, in summary, "Setting." The student was prompted by the video's mid-century images to investigate the history of the song and its historical context. Not only were these inquiries investigated, the student continued to inquire about race relations in the late 1990s. While the student's prose was the bear minimum required, it was packed with ideas and investigative process promoted by the instructions. One of the group topics regarding historical context was called "Construct a Historical Overview of the Video and Outside Influences." Like the solo student, this group was prompted by the video's images as a springboard into a discussion of history. The group isolated the video's connection to both 1993 and the mid-century, but they stopped short of any other real investigation. Instead, they allowed a couple of hollow assumptions about the identities of the people in the video and the videographer's intent to fill the remaining discussion space that was intended for a different purpose.

4. **Music:** Most, but not all, students and student groups had at least one music-centered topic. In addition to the instructions, I made a point in class to reiterate that including at least one music-centered topic was, indeed, required and necessary in a course like this. In this category, four general topics were prominent, and they are arranged here by decreasing popularity: musical genre, instrumentation, singing style, and rhythm/tempo. In this category, I also included the few topic submissions that referred to a connection between music and lyrics, as none of the topic submissions in the "Lyrics" category refer to the music in any way. I believe the topic submissions in this category were some of the most carefully researched, and they contained some of the best open-ended discussions. Two sample topics involving music were (1) exploring jazz and (2) exploring the connection between the music and the text.

One of the solo topics regarding music was called "Instrumentation." The student made a connection between this song and jazz, and subsequent investigation led to noting that the predominant use of strings in this song is unlike what is common in a jazz ensemble. The inquiry also led to finding the original 1967 version of the song, and then comparing its instrumentation to a standard jazz ensemble, as well as the later 1993 arrangement. One of the group topics regarding music was called "Instruments Used." While the solo and group topics are essentially the same, the results of the group's investigations were not as fruitful. The group did not provide as much prose, suggesting less inquiry and investigation. An important difference between the solo and the group was the group's commentary suggesting different instrumentations affect listeners in different ways. Inquiry that opens the discussion to music psychology is a fine avenue to follow; however, the group only offered cursory statements that were not connected to documented investigations.

PBL Outcomes and Assessment: Unit 1 Self-Assessment

After completing the Group/Solo Assessment, each student was instructed to complete a Self-Assessment Survey on their own. Interestingly, not everyone who completed the Group/Solo Assessment also completed the Self-Assessment Survey, and not everyone who completed the Self-Assessment Survey answered all six questions. To avoid confusion between these numerical differences, percentages are given instead of student numbers. Here are the questions and summaries of students' answers:

1. **Why did you decide to work in a self-selected group or work alone? Explain your answer.**

   Every student was encouraged to explain why they chose to work alone or in a group up to three members, and many listed more than one reason. Half of the students worked alone, and here are the main reasons why they chose to do so: 70% thought it would be easier to work alone, 45% stated they did not want to deal with others' schedules to find time to work, 40% did not know anyone in class well enough to want to work with them, and 25% stated a negative past experience with group work that influenced their decision. Half of the students worked in as a pair or trio, and here are the main reasons why they chose to do so: 77% thought it would be easier to work in a group, 69% wanted to work with others for increased input, and 31% had already established similar interests with another/others prior to the course or during the first two weeks of the course.

2. **Did you complete the assignments to the best of your abilities? If so, or if not, explain your work habits.**

   Of the half that worked alone, 65% reported to have done the best they could; 15% reported doing the best they could, although they had unresolved questions along the way; 15% reported they could have done better; and 10% reported that they did what they could, given the confusing nature of the assessment. Of the half that worked in a group, 38% reported to have done the best they could, 54% reported that the group helped them to do the best they could, and 8% reported that they could have done better.

3. **If you worked in a group, answer 3a, and if you worked by yourself, answer 3b:**

   3a – What did you contribute to your group?

   Of the half that worked in a group, everyone described presenting and discussing ideas, 29% also mentioned making sure the group was on task, and 8% mentioned supporting team members.

   3b – Looking back at your performance, what were your best moments in terms of productivity and positive results? Explain your answer.

   Of the half that worked alone, everyone described focused study, 35% added a statement about repeated listening to and watching the video without mentioning the writing process, 20% mentioned the writing process without mentioning listening to and viewing the video, and one person mentioned discussing the project with others.

4. **If you worked in a group, answer 4a, and if you worked by yourself, answer 4b:**

   4a – How could you have contributed more to your group, and why do you think this may be helpful? (or) If you could not have contributed more to your group, how could you have helped someone else in your group without doing work for them? (or) If everything was perfectly balanced, please explain what that experience was like.

   Of the half that worked in a group, 64% would change nothing, 21% felt the group did not have enough time to work together, 8% said they could have contributed more, and 8% described their inexperience with group work as a negative factor.

   4b – Looking back at your performance, what do you wish you would have done differently, if anything? Explain your answer.

   Of the half that worked alone, 60% thought they should have devoted more time to the assessment, 20% thought they should have asked the instructor more questions, 20% thought they should have researched more, 15% thought they should have utilized previous lectures more, 15% would change nothing, and 10% thought they should have worked in a group.

5. **If you worked in a group, answer 5a, and if you worked by yourself, answer 5b:**

   5a – How did you respond to contributions offered or not offered by others in your group?

   Of the half that worked in a group, everyone described a positive experience, where ideas and questions were freely discussed. One person added that they learned to value the input of others more.

   5b – Describe your emotional experience working with yourself on this unit, i.e. describe the possible fluctuation of your motivation level and your emotional responses to the tasks at hand.

   Of the half that worked alone, 30% stated that their motivation was generally low throughout because they either did not enjoy writing or the music studied; 25% were motivated because they value music; 25% remarked that their motivation increased as their research increased, even if they did not like the actual music being studied; 10% saw an increase in motivation once they began using prior experiences with music as a guide; and 10% felt their motivation would have been higher if they had worked in a group.

6. **If you worked in a group, answer 6a, and if you worked by yourself, answer 6b:**

   6a – Take a look at what is coming next in this course. In terms of music appreciation as you know it, do you think you want to continue in a group setting in the future, i.e. what was beneficial and/or what wasn't beneficial about your group setting? Please explain your answer, knowing that this question is meant to be open-ended.

   Of the half that worked in a group, 79% wanted to continue to work in a group, and 21% wanted to try going solo. Of those who wanted to continue working in a group, 82% mentioned that it made problem-solving easier, while one person mentioned it made dealing with procrastination easier. The 21% who wanted to try going solo were simply curious about what that experience in this course would be like.

   6b – Take a look at what is coming next in this course. In terms of music appreciation as you know it, do you think you want to continue without a group setting in the future, i.e. what was beneficial and/or what wasn't beneficial about your solo setting? Please explain your answer, knowing that this question is meant to be open-ended.

   Of the half that worked alone, 45% wanted to try working in a group, 30% wanted to continue to work alone, and 25% were undecided. Of those who wanted to try working in a group, 89% stated that group problem-solving is appealing to them and 22% stated that group work might help them become more motivated. Of those who wanted to continue to work alone, 67% believe working alone is the most efficient way to work, and 33% mentioned in-class discussion and the instructor as being useful resources. Those who were undecided reported the benefits of both group and solo work as being different, yet equally valuable.

Evaluation of the PBL Unit Assessments

When the assessments were first announced during the fourth class session, the students' overall response was positive. Perhaps this was because the previous lectures seemed to go smoothly, save a few disagreements regarding topic discussions. Also, the succinct nature of the instructions did not seem to immediately induce a stress response. During the sixth class session devoted to working on the Group/Solo Assessment, I could tell students began to realize that the assessment was asking for more work than they had anticipated because of its open-ended nature, demand for creativity, and focus on the research process. Many had little experience with open-ended assignments, and this sense of newness was made more profound by the fact that most were not used to constructing a web of appreciation for a piece of music.

For me, there were two great moments of success in the Group/Solo Assessment. The first great success was students' exposure to what music appreciation can encompass, coupled with a beginning experience of the work it takes to deeply appreciate a musical object. The second great success, though it was not realized by all, was the creation of at least one appreciation topic based on musical content. While students were coming to terms with what music appreciation means, they also had to come to terms with one or more of the following situations: their lack of experience with musical objects, their discomfort with formulating potentially unanswered questions about music, or their lack of interest in the musical object and/or creating appreciation of it. A failure shared by many students was the lack of recorded research in their topic discussions. Students seemed to be more interested in finding answers to their questions/topics than keeping track of all that they had done to derive their "answers." The instructions clearly state the priority of research over "definite answers," and this created confusion for some. Compared to the Group/Solo Assessment, students had few and unremarkable problems with the Self-Assessment Survey.

I would assign the Group/Solo Assessment again, as both I and students found it to be an informative measurement of students' ability to consider and create music appreciation in the early stage of an introductory course with no music prerequisites. It is a dynamic assessment that encouraged the development of inter- and intrapersonal skills during the discovery, interaction, research, and exploration processes as they pertain to music. The next time I assign this assessment, I will make some adjustments that will hopefully lead to a stronger sense of security and achievement among students. I will revise the instructions to give a clearer picture of what is required and how it is to be formatted without losing the assessment's open-ended nature. The biggest counterproductive trend was students' preoccupation with the specifically stated minimum requirement of four complete sentences per topic discussion. It may be more beneficial to also provide a topic model with the instructions, with the topic model containing an ordered list of all the required parts for easy reference. I would also like to use the instructions and the topic model as a means to place more emphasis on topic research and investigation that necessitate even longer topic explanations. I would follow the Group/Solo Assessment with the Self-Assessment Survey as it currently stands. Being able to curate appreciation of music as an independent learner also requires a strong reflective process in order to manage one's sense of motivation, achievement, and growth. I feel the Self-Assessment Survey successfully inspired introspection and self-awareness that students could also apply to other areas of study.

Part II
Ethnomusicology

6

Toward Integrating Problem-Based Learning in an Ethnomusicology Curriculum: Case Study with the Music Traditions of Africa Course

GAVIN WEBB

In the first of our ethnomusicology-centered chapters, Gavin applies his Problem-based inquiry in an upper division course on African music. His Problem-based Learning is designed to lead students into a deeper understanding of one of six regions of Africa by having them adopt an "insider" perspective. Students' final presentations must "represent" their particular area of the continent in a way that addresses centuries of "mis-representations" and misunderstandings. Gavin also requires intensive scholarly work to support their presentations, a component which is often overlooked in such projects.

If you like things easy, you'll have difficulties, if you like problems, you'll succeed.

—Routledge Book of World Proverbs (2006)

~

From 2000 until 2012, I worked in the field of international education running fully accredited study abroad programs in Africa in a few different capacities. While based at the Institute for African Studies within the University of Ghana, I was an Academic Director overseeing a cohort of anywhere from 20 to 30 students per semester delivering field-based programming to participants interested in language learning, the arts, and in the opportunity to carry out mentored fieldwork. As an Associate Dean, I oversaw a portfolio of cross-disciplinary programs across the African continent. The organization I served in these capacities was deeply committed to an experiential education model. Experiential education traces its roots back to John Dewey and has been defined as "a philosophy and methodology in which educators purposely engage learners in direct experience and focused reflection in order to increase knowledge, develop skills and clarify values" (2) (Smith & Knapp, p. 2). Perhaps out of ignorance, as a young Academic Director fresh out of graduate school, I didn't fully appreciate how progressive this pedagogical approach was, and I often glossed over this feature of our program when interacting with faculty members from US universities visiting my program in Ghana. In 2012, I made the leap from running international education programs in Africa to serving Binghamton University as a Visiting Assistant Professor in Ethnomusicology in Upstate New York. The transition from the field to the classroom was a bumpy one for me indeed. But what struck me after several interactions with the Center for Teaching and Learning (CTL) on campus was the way they embraced active learning strategies in general and experiential education in particular as a way to build more compelling classrooms and better engage students. Resource people from the CTL were very eager to support faculty working toward incorporating these types of instructional methods into their classrooms. So, I was very excited to be invited to participate in this initiative to develop models, guidelines, best practices, and assessment tools for Problem-based Learning (PBL) instructional methods in the music curriculum.

In what follows, I discuss the application of the PBL instructional model to my Music Traditions of Africa course. After presenting contextual and course-specific information, I present an overview of the PBL project that I integrated into my course. I conclude my chapter with an overview of the outcomes, a review of the students' assessment of the PBL component of the course, and suggest how my findings can contribute to our understanding of the lesser-studied issue of the nature of problem types. Ethnomusicology is inherently interdisciplinary and encompasses many different approaches; however, the construction of musical meaning in the study of a music culture requires a problem formulation that is interpretive in design.

Course Information

As an instructional method developed for the medical sciences, I was concerned that PBL would not be an ideal approach to any of the courses in my portfolio, which cover the theory and method of ethnomusicology, and survey the musical and cultural traditions of Africa, the African Diaspora, and Asia. Ethnomusicologists are not designing bridges or diagnosing patients but applying the tools of music theory and ethnographic inquiry to interpret and construct musical meaning in cultures around the world.

To apply the PBL pedagogy to one of my courses, I selected *Music Traditions of Africa* (MUS/AFST 380), a course that tends to attract upper-level undergraduates and has an average enrollment of 15–20 students. Music Traditions of Africa engages the entire continent and all dimensions of music production and performance, including popular music, styles connected with particular ethno-linguistic traditions, music associated with various forms of spiritual expression, and to a limited extent, art music traditions as well. While the course is primarily delivered through investigating geographic clusters, attention is also explicitly devoted to looking at music from analytical perspectives as well, such as the relationship between music and identity or the essential connection between music and spirituality or healing.

MUS 380/AFST 380A meets for 90 minutes each Tuesday and Thursday and attracts both "A" and "C" general education designations – Aesthetics and Composition, respectively. The Composition component requires me to devote significant attention to the process of scholarly writing, with students submitting major writing assignments requiring substantive revision based on my feedback. This somewhat limits the way I organize the course, and was an important consideration I had to take into account as I revised the course curriculum to accommodate the PBL pedagogy. Many students also select MUS 380/AFST 380A as it helps fulfill their major/minor in Africana Studies.

As it is a course taught with the spirit of ethnomusicological practices and approaches in mind, the content and delivery is cross-disciplinary in scope. In addition to its primary focus on music, the class engages issues connected with history, politics, African studies, postcolonial and religious studies, cultural and Diaspora studies, as well as human migration. I felt that the broad yet critical approach to the course content was most congruent with the PBL pedagogy, whereby students could confront real and current "problems" facing Africa and the study of her music and culture.

I took several considerations into account in developing the course learning outcomes. For example, outcomes connected with the general education requirements and that of the course more broadly. Upon successful completion of the course, students could expect be able to:

General Education Outcomes

- Demonstrate understanding of course content through formal academic writing
- Construct effective prose that demonstrates critical thinking and advances sound conclusions, appropriate to the course and discipline
- Demonstrate the ability to revise and improve one's writing in both form and content
- Demonstrate an understanding of the creative process and the role of imagination and aesthetic judgement in at least one principal form of artistic expression in such fields as art, art history, cinema, creative writing, dance, graphic design, music, and theater.

Course-Specific Outcomes

- Demonstrate understanding of regional idiosyncrasies in Africa with respect to musical style, genre, instrumentation, cultural and spiritual influence, and historical experience

- Demonstrate the capacity to think critically about the relationship between music and culture
- Demonstrate understanding of the core issues ethnomusicological research engages in the study of African music.

The Problem-Based Learning Project

Serious ethnomusicologists working in Africa, particularly those from metropolitan locales, often contend with a number of challenges. While many of these challenges likely resonate with scholars or musicians working in other postcolonial societies, they manifest in a particular way in the context of Africa. Some of these issues include asymmetrical power relations and levels of material wealth between the researcher and the researched, the history of racism, colonial legacies and neocolonial realities, poor understanding of Africa in the metropolis, poor understanding of African languages among researchers, metropolitan dominance of scholarly production, etc. The PBL project sought to expose students to these and many other challenges, and engage a selection of texts that have attempted to assess Africanist ethnomusicology from a critical and postcolonial perspective.

Since the overwhelming majority of my students have little knowledge of African music, the course demanded that attention be devoted to providing a survey of the salient musical and cultural features of each of the continent's regions. As a result, I made the decision to divide the course into two units. The first section began with the course orientation and overview of the principles and procedures of ethnomusicology, and then concentrated on providing students with a regional survey of the musical and cultural features of Africa, typically on the Tuesday of each week. Thursdays were devoted to formal discussion of Kofi Agawu's contentious book *Representing African Music: Post-Colonial Notes, Queries, Positions* (2003) and select articles that complimented or interrogated its scope and content (Meintjes 2006 and Erlmann 2006). Despite the fact that some ethnomusicologists working in Africa have engaged postcolonial analytical perspectives in print, Agawu's book represents the most comprehensive and reflective critique of ethnomusicology's relationship to the evolving forms of colonialism in Africa, the misrepresentation of the continent and its people, and the perpetuation of power asymmetries.

The second half of the course was more specifically devoted to the PBL projects. Students formed groups and selected a region of Africa to work with – e.g. West Africa, Southern Africa, East Africa, Central Africa, or North Africa. Working in groups, I asked students to develop projects interrogating the following assertion:

Africa and its music have endured centuries of misrepresentation, misunderstanding, and misinformation that has distorted understanding of the continent and its people. Assess the validity of this statement.

Students were then required to:

1. Give a class presentation (20–30 minutes) providing an overview of the musical and cultural features of the region and assessing the statement based on various forms of "text" – websites, scholarly books or journals, YouTube links, travel media, podcasts, blogs, etc. Each group is required to demonstrate advanced understanding of their region by devoting a significant portion of their time to working with scholarly sources
2. Submit a 500-word statement distilling each group's main findings
3. Develop the materials and select a format for presenting them. In addition to assessing the statement, these materials should function as a shared resource for the class to further engage other regions of African than their own, and so a significant portion of the grade will be assigned each group's ability to do this well.

Although the course was imagined as two distinct units, the PBL assignment was presented from the beginning of the semester with benchmarks built into the syllabus to keep each group on track. This was done to avoid last-minute panicking and the submission of superficial assignments. The benchmarks intended to guide the students through the essential steps of problem-solving, from doing research, to assessing their findings, and finally to developing solutions by applying what they had learned:

• Weeks 2–6: Conducting Research: Formulating the Problem and

Collecting Data

• Weeks 7–9: Integrating Theory and Practice: Assessing the Representation of African Music in Your Region and Generating Hypotheses about Solutions
• Weeks 10–12: Applying Your Knowledge: Developing Solutions to the Representation of African Music

Process of Implementation

From Weeks 8 to 12, each Tuesday class session was designated to the PBL, allowing time for students to work independently within their groups. As I transitioned from professor to facilitator from the first half to the second half of the semester, I made use of these sessions to move around the classroom to offer support or assess their progress. Thursday classes were earmarked for practical dance sessions or to engage an analytical perspective related to the study of music in Africa.

Case Study Outcomes

I allowed each group to create their own vehicle for presenting their materials, and as a result, there were a few different types of presentation formats for each of the regions. Below is a summary of the results from the Spring 2017 semester.

North Africa

The group with the most comprehensive presentation of their region and the most nuanced understanding of the representation issues was those working in the North Africa region. Students presented their findings through creation of a WordPress page – Northafricanmusic.wordpress.com – where they provided a historical overview of their region and presented a selection of important music types and cultures such as Berber music and culture, Andalusian music, Malouf, and Rai. They then discussed the importance of Islam in the region, Malouf music, Andalusian music, Rai, Tunisian Underground, Nubian music, and Chaabi. Students also included a section, "Representing African Music," that looked primarily at issues of nomenclature and discussed some of the innovations coming from the continent.

West Africa

The most ambitious group was the one representing West Africa. While they covered a lot of material, they paid less attention to effectively presenting it. In the end, they distributed the salient features of their region to the class through a PowerPoint presentation, in which they presented a thesis – that "traditional music" has a deeply contemplative dimension and that popular music from Africa has indeed been well represented in music scholarship. This was impressive since it was an argument presented by Agawu whereby he suggests that European scholars have tended toward describing African music in functional terms or giving primacy to the social setting that grounds the performance type in contrast to European music scholarship which doesn't have this burden placed upon it (Agawu 2003, 98). They also discussed regional influences and some of the cultural features of West Africa, such as instrumentation, important musicians, and a series of "case studies" that examined select music types from Nigeria, Ghana, and to a lesser extent Liberia. Their oral presentation sought to embody the communal spirit of African musical practices through a "hands-on" component to their presentation that included some performances and inviting willing members of the class to learn a dance.

East Africa

The East Africa region's final product included an informational pamphlet in support of their oral presentation. Comprising one page of information and graphics on the front and back, it included a list of the countries found in the subregion, some features of Kenyan and Ethiopian history (the focus of their presentation), a discussion of religious features, pictures capturing important cultural features, and a translation of "happy birthday" in Swahili.

Southern Africa

As their peers did in North Africa, the group representing southern Africa presented their material through WordPress – https://southafricanmusic. wordpress.com/. There, they sought to provide a comprehensive overview of the music and cultures from the region, including South Africa, Botswana, Angola, Mozambique, Zimbabwe, and Madagascar. In each of these countries, they gave a brief overview of the historical and cultural features, discussed some aspects of instrumentation, and selected some musical examples as representative of each.

Central Africa

The group representing Central Africa created a "travel brochure" which they distributed to the class via Google Docs. Their presentation covered Angola, Equatorial Guinea, and the Congo. Each of these sections included a "regional overview," a discussion about some of the cultural features, a brief discussion of history, a look at the main music cultures found, and a discussion of representational issues. Each member took responsibility for one country, so what resulted was a somewhat lopsided view of the region depending on the input of the student.

Assessment

At the completion of the course, students were asked to respond to seven questions designed to assess the PBL component. To compel the students to participate, I offered extra credit for those who completed the task. All students in the class submitted their responses, which I've distilled here for the purposes of reflecting on the possible value of PBL approaches to ethnomusicology. In total, I was able to collect responses from 17 students, including one student from a previous semester who offered feedback based on the same set of questions. While I asked students to answer each question separately, several of them submitted responses comprised of continuous prose. As a result, it is possible that some of the questions were not clearly answered or were missed altogether which affected my response rates.

Did you benefit from the group work?

82% of the respondents answered this question in the affirmative. Students identified a range of reasons why they felt the group work was beneficial. One respondent suggested that the "different perspectives of my group forced my mind to open up. In my group we had a whole bunch of different majors, dance, math, African studies, and biology," citing the cross-disciplinary nature of the students which enriched their collective orientation to the problem. Others confirmed that group work allows members to "share ideas" or "get new perspectives on our assignment from the people I worked with," or "to develop new ways of working with people." Of the respondents to this question, 35% (5 out of 14 – a mix of both positive and negative respondents) expressed negative experiences in past group project learning environments, citing the common challenge of an unequal distribution of effort put into completing tasks among members. While this is to be expected to some degree, I added a peer evaluation component to the students' overall assessment that was intended to mitigate it. Nevertheless, negative respondents to this question cited this as a primary reason for why they did not benefit from the PBL method – "some students never come to class [during the group working sessions]," "mainly I did the work," and "Group projects are notorious for being completely unfair."

How effective were the PBL class sessions where you worked independently in your groups? Did you get stuff done, or was it a waste of time? If so, why?

Students were less enthusiastic about the class sessions devoted to working on their projects in groups, and only 57% of respondents felt positive about this component (4 out of 7 students who responded). A foundational feature of the PBL approach, this was to be the moment where my role transformed from professor to that of a mentor or tutor as I went around the room toward the end of the session to monitor their progress, help troubleshoot, identify resources, reframe issues they were struggling with, suggest ideas about presenting materials, provide general motivation, etc. Several students responded favorably to my shifting role in the classroom. Some of the reasons students responded positively include that it was tough to meet outside of class due to conflicting schedules, it was a time in the week that the group could track their progress, or that it was a time where students could bounce ideas off each other more easily. Others disagreed, citing that their group didn't get much done during these sessions (no explanations as to why this happened), or that the classroom became too noisy thereby making it difficult to concentrate or work effectively. Two student responses felt that too much time was devoted to these sessions, with one of the two suggesting that this time in the course could have been better directed toward covering course materials.

Did you appreciate the approach, or were you looking for a "more traditional" type of course delivery?

I asked students to consider whether or not they would have preferred a more "traditional" approach to delivering the course materials over the PBL instructional model. 76% of respondents suggested that they appreciated the PBL approach to the course (10 out of 13). Students cited the fact that they were able to focus on a specific subregion and therefore deepen their knowledge of a specific area, that the group work allowed them to meet new people, that it provided some relief from other classes that are lecture heavy, that it allowed people to do independent research on a topic of interest, or that it offered students with different learning styles an opportunity to excel. Two students who respondent positively did so with some caveats. One student was interested in more assignments that engaged the required readings, while the other student felt that more attention should be devoted to introducing students to African music from a practical perspective through learning songs, dances, or various instruments. Two of the students who responded negatively felt that the PBL method was flawed since students coming into the course lack even a basic understanding of music and culture from the continent, and so to ask them to interrogate whether or not scholarship on music from the continent has been misrepresented is problematic.

Do you feel you have a solid understanding of the various genres, instruments, historical processes, and cultural features of music from different parts of Africa?

As I was concerned that the PBL assignment would get in the way of achieving some of the intended outcomes for the course, I asked students to evaluate whether or not they felt the course adequately covered important cultural, musical, and historical features of Africa. 70% of respondents answered positively (7 out of 10). As mentioned earlier, groups were partly evaluated on their project's ability to function as a shared resource for the rest of the students in the class. Out of the seven students who responded positively, four mentioned this as an important part of their understanding of musical traditions and cultures from different parts of the continent. Of the three students that responded negatively, one cited the PBL instructional method specifically as being a barrier to adequate understanding of the musical and cultural features of African music: "I understand certain things regarding African music better than before taking the class. I do think I would have learned more had the class been organized in a more traditional manner."

What worked well?

When asked "what worked well," students responded in a variety of ways – some were linked to the PBL project specifically, while others were connected with activities or assignments related to the class. There were a few general trends, however, that can be gleaned from the feedback. The class sessions and the times where I would move between the different groups to offer support were made mention of by three and two students, respectively (at this point, recall that both of these features of the PBL project were also mentioned as a positive feature of the method for other questions). For example, one student responded, "The classes where we worked on the project during class was very helpful. What was especially helpful was talking to you about any concerns and your help in better navigating it. I feel like talking to you made us better understand what you were asking of us and helped put us on a better path. When we had our group meetings outside of class, we worked the same way we did in class but it was definitely more helpful having your assistance."

What didn't work well?

In the spirit of working each semester to improve upon the previous, I asked students to outline what they felt didn't work well for the PBL component. As with the feedback on what worked well, I received responses (seven in total) that were also connected with other components of the course. With respect to feedback on the PBL portion specifically, students responded by suggesting that they felt inadequate time was allotted for presentations, that one of the groups was too small (three students compared to five in the others), thereby making it tough to go into greater detail, and that the different skills and abilities among group members made it tough to effectively present as a group.

What could I have done to improve the PBL component?

When asked what I could have done to improve the PBL project, the answers once again varied widely. Students suggested a range of improvements, from working with groups to better present the materials by adding more visual and multimedia components, to begin the PBL projects earlier in the semester, allot more time for group presentations, to better focusing the problem, and to giving groups more guidance on possible research materials at the beginning of the semester so that they can have more time for analyzing their data.

Reflection and Analysis

As PBL continues to migrate to other academic disciplines, research needs to consider the nature of the problems being solved and how efficacious PBL methodologies are for those kinds of problems (Jonassen and hung, 2008, 8).

As I constructed the PBL design for this course, I anchored it in what I felt would be a compelling and appropriate ill-structured problem for my students to engage in. At the back of my mind, however, was a persistent concern that I was asking too much of the students, or that the materials I was asking them to engage were too abstract. I took solace in PBL's method that requires instructors to support students as they scaffold knowledge to fill gaps, thereby ideally, over the course of the project, equipping students with the requisite level of understanding to enable them to assess the validity of the statement.

Research into PBL approaches and methods has more recently sharpened its focus on the nature of the problems from which the instructional method is rooted. As Hung and Jonassen (2008) remind us, not all problems are equal, and the kinds of problems posited for students, as to be expected, vary quite widely from one discipline to another. My initial concern about the appropriateness of the problem for the class was nested inside the set of "internal factors" comprised of the capacities and experiences of the students in my class – level of domain knowledge, experience in solving problems, causal and analogical reasoning skills, and epistemological development (Jonassen and Hung 2008, 8). I was sure that my students came to the course with some experience solving problems systematically and using an appropriate epistemology. However, despite being a level 400 course, I knew many of my students came with little prior knowledge of African music or ethnomusicology and would need a lot of support to determine the causal factors that some scholars suggest lie at the heart of the misrepresentation of African music in scholarship. The PBL offered me an outlet to provide this support to students.

By contrast, there are a number of "external factors" that allow scholars to determine problem difficulty that I saw play out in the course of the PBL project. First is that of "complexity" – breadth of knowledge required, attainment level of domain knowledge, intricacy of problem-solution procedures, and relational complexity (Jonassen and Hung 2008). To illustrate, the nature of the problem I posed for students required them to reach into a number of disciplinary domains such as ethnomusicology, anthropology, or postcolonial studies and integrate factual information, concepts, and methods from them as they worked toward solving the problem. How intricate a problem is depends on the number of steps required to come to a solution, and in the course of my PBL project, students were required to compile data from a variety of scholarly sources to be able to vet the validity of the statement proposed, build knowledge of their subregion, analyze that data, and make a determination based on their findings. A comprehensive rendering of the problem also required students to come to grips with a broad number of analytical concepts in the multiple fields the research engaged, and therefore this required students to consider a "more relationally complex body of knowledge" (Jonassen and Hung 2008, 11).

Second is that of "strucutredness" (ibid) – intransparency, heterogeneity of interpretations, interdisciplinarity, dynamicity, and competing alternatives. While students entered the course and the PBL with multiple knowledge gaps, the content they engaged was nevertheless knowable or didn't contain a significant number of unknown variables. Multiple interpretations of the problem and the possible solutions that one could posit are important features of the project and added to the ill-structured nature of it. The parasitic nature of ethnomusicological inquiry means that it relies on an interdisciplinary approach, and its concern with the interpretation of musical meaning lends itself to multiple and completing interpretation of its findings.

Interpretation-Assessment Problems

With the nature of problem difficulty in mind, I am proposing a contribution to Jonassen's Typology of Problem types (2000) that heretofore has yet to integrate problems classes appropriate to ethnomusicological teaching, research, and learning. Jonassen's typology situates 11 problem classes along a well-structured to ill-structured continuum (right to left, however, represented below as top to bottom) (ibid, 74–75):

    i) Logical
    ii) Algorithmic
    iii) Story
    iv) Rule-using
    v) Decision-making
    vi) Troubleshooting
    vii) Diagnosis-solution
    viii) Strategic performance
    ix) Case analysis
    x) Design
    xi) Dilemmas

I propose that this problem class be referred to as *interpretation-assessment* problems and that along the continuum proposed by Jonassen lie between *case analysis* and *design* problems. Following Jonassen's identification and description of a problem's components that determine the level of abstractness and complexity (2000, 72–73), below I unpack these features that I feel lie at the heart of the *interpretation-assessment* problem class.

Interpretation-Assessment

Learning activity refers to the essential outcomes for a problem type, whereas *inputs* identifies what is put into operation in the course of the problem-solving process. How successful the solution is determined by the *Success criteria*, and as Jonassen (2000) suggests, problems that lie closer to the ill-structured end of the continuum place more emphasis on "decision articulation and argumentation" rather than "correct, efficient solutions." *Context* identifies the degree of the outcome's importance in the case of ill-structured problems, whereas well-structured ones tend toward more abstract forms of results. The structuredness of a problem depends on the "transparency, stability, and predictability" of the problem (Jonassen and Hung, 2008, 11), and *abstractness*

Table 6.1 Assessment Criteria

Learning Activity	Identifying resources, assessing data, applying findings and structuring positions
Inputs	Position constrained by discipline with multiple interpretations
Success Criteria	Multiple possibilities, evidence clearly articulated
Context	Real world, interdisciplinary, complex
Structuredness	Ill-structured
Abstractness	Issue situated

refers to the reasoning skills that are employed in problem-solving which are "domain-and-context-specific" (Jonassen 2000, 68) (Table 6.1).

The inclusion of *interpretation-assessment* problems into this typology opens up a space for domains of inquiry such as ethnomusicology that, while grounded in analytical and critical approaches, are interpretive and dialogic in their orientation. This is not to say that ethnomusicologists don't grapple with problems that can have viable and clear solutions, and one must acknowledge how subfields like applied ethnomusicology seek application of its findings to real-world challenges, but Jonassen's 2000 typology fails to include a type of problem construction that engages students in a process of solution finding which can't be readily assessed as factually true or false. Good PBL projects that sought to answer the validity of the statement I proposed were required to have sufficient evidence presented in order to validate their positions, but in the end, the project presentations were about generating dialogue within the class and pushing students one step closer to good critical thinking about the nature of the scholarly representation of music from Africa.

Conclusion

For professors committed to finding opportunities to transform their classrooms and embrace active learning strategies, PBL will continue to be an important option among the different instructional models available. It has grown substantially over the past 50+ years since emerging in the 1960s in Canadian medical schools, so that today disciplines such as engineering, business, and mathematics find this approach useful to train students. Student feedback and the assessment of student projects suggest that my own experiment with implementing PBL into an ethnomusicology course can result in positive outcomes for students and yield interesting results. My own assessment of the nature of the problem in the latter part of this study suggests that there is a gap in the typology posited by Jonassen (2000) that are at the core of PBL, and that the integration of *interpretation-assessment* problems into the typology enriches its scope and could encourage the application of PBL to disciplines such as the interpretive sciences in general, and ethnomusicology in particular.

Bibliography

Agawu, Kofi. *Representing African Music: Postcolonial Notes, Queries, Positions.* New York: Routledge, 2003.

Erlmann, Veit. "Resisting Sameness: À propos Kofi Agawu's Representing African Music." *Music Theory Spectrum* 26, no. 2 (2004): 291–304.

Jonassen, David H. "Toward a Design Theory of Problem Solving." *Educational Technology Research and Development* 48, no. 4 (2000): 63–85.

Jonassen, David H. and Woei Hung. "All Problems are Not Equal: Implications for Problem-Based Learning." *Interdisciplinary Journal of Problem-Based Learning* 2 no. 2 (2008): 6–28.

Meintjes, Louise. "Representing African Music: Postcolonial Notes, Queries, Positions by Kofi Agawu." *Journal of the American Musicological Society* 59, no. 3 (2006): 769–77.

Smith, Thomas E. and Clifford E. Knapp, eds. *Sourcebook of Experiential Education: Key Thinkers and their Contributions.* New York: Routledge, 2011.

Stone, Jon R. *The Routledge Book of World Proverbs.* New York: Routledge, 2006.

7
Diversity and Collaboration in Modern Africa and in the (Mostly) Online Classroom

TIFFANY NICELY

Our second ethnomusicology offering also includes Africa as a culture area as well as issues concerning hybrid learning. In this chapter, Tiffany describes the Problem-Based Learning approach as "purposeful open-endedness" and sees the process of PBL as mirroring the processes of cooperation found in many African communities. Her "Your Country" PBL also takes advantage of this open-endedness in that it is impossible to solve and requires students to seek information, form assessments, and create blurbs for their adopted country far beyond what is accessible on the Internet. Intergroup feedback and reflections are required along the way, and at the end of the chapter, Tiffany provides a description of what she would do differently when she re-implements the PBL.

~

I was tasked with creating MUS 209, Sub-Saharan African Music and Cultures, at State University of New York (SUNY) Buffalo State in 2009 to fill a gap in the college's non-Western civilizations offerings and further diversify the music department's electives. As I developed this course, I drew on my background as a performer of multiple West African and Diasporic drumming styles and as a theoretician whose research focuses on analytical approaches to polyrhythm. I also built on my experiences having taught World Music Cultures for several semesters. Since 2009, I have taught both courses every semester.

The first thing that drew me to Problem-Based Learning (PBL) was my ongoing search for engaging teaching methodologies and opportunities to improve my teaching routine. What appealed to me most about the philosophy was its purposeful open-endedness. Students tend to want to know what the "right" answer is and the quickest way to get there – often memorizing a short list of items to regurgitate and then quickly flush out of their memories. I am always looking for new ways to help them realize that one of the greatest strengths of any art form is its openness to interpretation and nuance. Music is essential to every culture because it encapsulates some of our most core human attributes: cooperation, individuality, and complexity via multiple overlapping meanings. I welcomed a teaching philosophy that begins with the premise that the real-world problems we take on are fundamentally unsolvable, allowing us to focus on the process of discovery, skill building, and decision-making.

In the fall of 2017, I implemented a PBL project in both sections of my Sub-Saharan African Music and Cultures class, with the guiding question "How does traditional, popular, and national music of Africa reflect the values, experiences, and needs of the people who use it?" I decided to use PBL to address two challenges I routinely face in teaching this course: the divergent background knowledge and skills of students taking the course and a disconnect between the students and the music we study in class. I was also hoping to draw on PBL's simulation of constrained collaboration that is central to the postcolonial African condition, which manifests in politics and cultural expressions including music.

Background

MUS 209, Sub-Saharan African Music and Cultures, fulfills a Non-Western Civilization requirement at SUNY Buffalo State. Through this course, students learn about African history and culture, using music as the specific lens through which to explore human expression. Prior knowledge of Africa, music, and African music varies widely among students who register for this class, and the 52 students who took MUS 209 in the fall semester of 2017 fell into the following subsets: (1) music majors who want to take a non-Western civilizations course that incorporates music but generally arrive with no content-specific knowledge of African music (eight students); (2) nonmusic majors who have a special interest in Africa and generally arrive with a good deal of prior knowledge about some facet of African history or culture, including several second-generation African immigrants (12 students); and (3) nonmusic majors with no prior knowledge of African history or culture (the remaining 32 students). As with all classes but perhaps exacerbated by these types of particular specialist knowledge – music and African culture – my overarching course-wide challenge is to teach these divergent populations, guiding each student from their individual starting places to a collective destination comprised of wider knowledge, understanding, and enhanced skills.

I teach MUS 209 as a hybrid, consisting of a traditional lecture format as well as online learning. We meet in person a total of eight times during the semester, with most of the information delivered and coursework completed online using Blackboard – the course management software licensed by Buffalo State. While I use an African Studies textbook, *The African Experience*, by Vincent Khapoya, for the historical and sociological overview, I supply all of the musical terms and concepts used in the class. My hybrid course is set up so that students work on their own time to gain exposure to and gather facts via the textbook as well as through historical documentary music example mp3's and videos I have posted on Blackboard. Online reading questions and open-ended essay prompts accompany each of these online learning tools. I use our face-to-face meetings for large- and small-group discussions to teach in more depth about African music and to give quizzes and exams.

The course is organized into four units. Each unit covers a period of sub-Saharan history and the music of one region. Within each unit, students complete one part of what I call the "Your Country" project. Every semester, I assign each student a country on which to focus for a series of assignments. This gives each student the opportunity to balance the general information they are learning in the course as a whole with knowledge of a specific set of people and circumstances. I chose to implement PBL into the "Your Country" project.

Project Implementation

Modern-day Africa presents a host of what Savery (2006) calls "ill-structured problems," which he considers a requirement for true PBL. The continent is made up of countries largely created during the colonial period of the mid- to late twentieth century, a process that both forced together disparate ethnic groups and separated others. Culture is further divided along religious lines, with traditional animist/ancestor belief systems overlaid with and often at odds with varying interpretations of Islam and Christianity. Finally, the contrast between traditional life in rural villages, where most people are still subsistence farmers, and growing globally aware urban centers creates issues of national cohesion. I would argue that the vast and diverse musics made on this continent reflect some of the ways in which people work together and show mutual respect, employing "real-world PBL."

A recurring challenge I have faced when teaching both African and world music classes in American colleges for the past ten years is that many students exhibit a disconnect between the music they love and music that they learn about in the classroom. Many of my students show up to class with earbuds in and music playing. When I ask what music means to them and what they use it for, many of them respond that it is essential to their happiness and has a place in most of their daily lives, which they accompany with a different playlist for every situation. Yet many of these same students show disdain or apathy toward musics of other cultures, or perhaps more to the point, they confuse personal taste with value. I seek to bridge this gap in two ways in my classes: first, by showing how the music of various cultures fulfills the same needs and functions that it does for my students (mood enhancement, recreation, social bonding, ritual), and second, by consistently including popular music in my regional music class presentations, I show my respect for popular music while opening their eyes and ears to the variety of popular music being made in the world. I incorporated both of these strategies into my PBL assignment.

I chose to implement PBL within the "Your Country" project, inviting students to apply their disparate preexisting knowledge and experience in a group setting. As mentioned previously, the group process of the PBL also mirrors the cooperation used in African culture and identifies the lack of a "single-right-answer" that modern Africans face every day. In addition, the PBL addresses a perceived "relation gap" between students and the subject matter. In implementing the PBL so, I had to give up some of my control and facilitate their discovery rather than giving it to them prepackaged.

MUS 209 Course Student Learning Outcomes

SUNY Student Learning Objective #2 for Other World Civilizations: Students will demonstrate knowledge of the distinctive features of the history, institutions, economy, society, culture, etc. of one non-Western civilization.

Buffalo State College Intellectual Foundations Student Learning Objective #2 for Other Word Civilizations: Students will analyze ways of thought in one or more historical period, in one or more other world civilization or multicultural region, including at least two foundational fields of thought (e.g. science and religion, or artistic expression and political philosophy).

MUS 209 Learning Objectives: Students will demonstrate knowledge of the following:

- A general outline of African history
- Three fundamental African musical elements: *patterns, polyrhythm,* and *improvisation*
- Analysis of African music via *sounds, settings,* and *significance*
- Specific ways in which modern Africa is a collection of recently created countries that bring together ethnic groups, traditions, and ideologies

Project Description

I implemented a PBL project as the final of four "Your Country" assignments in the fall semester of 2017. At the beginning of the semester, each student was assigned one African country on which to focus for a series of assignments, each requiring them to research-specific information about their country and the ethnic groups living there. Each student completed the first three assignments separately. First, they became acquainted with the basic facts of their country such as location, size, population by ethnicities, literacy rates, and health statistics. Many of these students have never heard of their assigned country, making this task critical to their basic understanding of the project. The next stage of the semester-long exploration of their country required students to focus on four ethnic groups living in their country, including questions about traditional day-to-day life, beliefs, and music. For the third assignment, students researched the colonial period. In previous semesters, the fourth and final installment of the "Your Country" assignment was a written report tying together this knowledge. However, I decided that the fourth installment of "Your Country" was the perfect place to attempt to implement a PBL. At this point, each student had become a comparative expert on a particular country, and bringing together multiple students with different perspectives, backgrounds, and opinions would invite a robust collaboration.

I divided the 52 students registered for my two sections of MUS 209 into 16 groups of two to five members based on their assigned countries. Some of the groups worked on only one country (DRC, Ghana, Nigeria, Ivory Coast), but most were made up of small "coalitions" of neighboring countries, such as Benin-Togo and Mali-Senegal. This assignment took place over the last four weeks of class, at the same time as students were completing their other Unit 4 assignments (reading questions and video responses for this unit). The bulk of their work on this project was due at the end of week 2, so I made it the only assignment due that week (Table 7.1).

This group project is open-ended and impossible to "solve" due to the restricted numbers of examples allowed in a website intended to represent the music of people of varied ethnic groups and ages. Also, I know from experience how difficult it can be to find detailed information on some areas of Africa. YouTube is a wonderful source of examples, but it generally lacks the types of concrete information required for this assignment, sending students on a quest to match information to music. Conversely, world music field recordings tend to be uneven in ethnic groups represented, and they simply cannot keep up with popular music the way popular media outlets do. Students dealt with these challenges by prioritizing and making decisions.

Table 7.1 PBL Group Website Assignment at a Glance

1. Site Plan	As a group, decide which four types of examples each group member will research. These must reflect a diversity of ethnic groups, a mixture traditional and popular music, and include the national anthem of each country represented by your group.
2. Examples and Blurbs	Each student provides links to audio or video for four examples as planned above, plus a 100- to 200-word text blurb describing the people, sound, setting, and significance of each example.
3. Intra-Group Feedback	Each student provides specific written feedback on at least four of their team members' examples and blurbs.
4. Reflection	Each student writes answers to four reflection questions about the entire semester-long "Your Country" assignment.

The Assignment

Your group has been hired by the cultural ministry of your country or coalition of countries. Your job is to create a website showcasing the music of your country by compiling musical examples and writing the text for the imagined website. Each group member is responsible for four musical examples and accompanying text blurbs, which taken together must include a fair distribution of your country's ethnic groups, and both traditional and popular musics. The national anthem of each country must also be included as one example. It is up to each group to decide how to plan and share information. You may use email, group chats, meet in person, or select another format that works for the group. The entire text must be in your own words, designed to be understandable to an American college student. This culminating assignment of the "Your Country" project comes at the end of the semester at which point each student has become an expert on their country. Utilize the knowledge you have gained, and go back to previous assignments for inspiration and material.

The completed website will have examples of and information on the following types of music (it is up to the group to determine how many slots to devote to each type):

1. **National anthem** of each coalition country
2. **Traditional music** of different ethnic groups
3. Multiple contrasting examples of current **popular music**

Informational blurbs about each example, written in your own words, must include:

1. **People**: who uses this music? As applicable, this should include ethnic group and age range
2. **Sound**: a description of the instruments and voices used, and the musical style. Include the use of patterns, polyrhythm, and improvisation as appropriate to each example
3. **Setting**: Where and when is this music used?
4. **Significance**: Why do people use this music? What does this music mean to specific performers and listeners?

Step One: Site Plan (Week 1/4)

Each group collaboratively determined what types of musical examples to include on their website, with the goal to reflect the ethnic diversity of their country or countries, and also represent traditional styles, current popular music, and the national anthem of each country. Site plans were submitted on Blackboard Learn as a single document listing each group member with the four musical example-types they would each research and write about.

Step Two: Musical Examples and Text Blurbs for Website (Week 2/4)

Each student selected four musical examples as agreed on in their site plan, and researched and wrote 100- to 200-word text blurbs about each one. The blurbs contained information on the people who make and listen to the music, with ethnic group details as applicable, as well as the three types of information as outlined by Kay Kaufman Shelemay in *Soundscapes* (an ethnomusicology textbook I use for a different class) regarding the *sound, setting,* and *significance* of each example.

With my encouragement, most students utilized YouTube to find their examples. Despite the fact that YouTube is not a peer-reviewed or what might be considered an "academic" resource, it has become an important source of videos of current music in Africa posted by Africans for the past several years. I also showed students other online databases such as those licensed by the school library, but YouTube proved to be the most useful, particularly for the popular music examples.

Throughout the semester, I modeled how to find and describe musical examples in this manner. My two in-class quizzes and two exams also include a musical identification section, where students select the country, ethnic group, and instrumentation of a sound clip that they have studied ahead of time. I demonstrate how to use web resources such as Smithsonian Folkways and BBC Radio "World on 3," and lead students through the process of aural analysis focusing on the three main musical elements explored in my class: patterns, polyrhythm, and improvisation.

Step Three: Intra-Group Feedback (Week 3/4)

Every group member was required to give feedback on at least four of their teammates' examples and text. Rather than having the goal of improving one another's writing, this was an opportunity to share reactions to and facilitate further discussion about the music and the people who use it. Each completed feedback response contained at least four sentences, based on the following feedback prompts: "I like the example you chose because...," "This music reminds me of... because...," "I like the way you described... because...," "based on what you wrote, I want to know more about...," and "You could have said more about...."

Step Four: Reflection (Week 4/4)

Individually, students answered four reflection questions about the entire "Your Country" series of assignments.

1. Before you took MUS 209, how much did you know about the country you worked on this semester? Please give your answer first as a number from 0 to 10 (zero prior knowledge to lot), and then write a few sentences about your prior knowledge of your country.
2. Over the course of the four "Your Country" assignments, what were at least three things that surprised you about your country?
3. This question refers to the process of completing the "Your Country" project. Write four to six sentences describing what it was like to research your country. Was information readily available? What sources did you use? What obstacles did you face in completing this assignment?
4. This course uses music as the lens through which to understand different African cultures. Write a brief essay (4–10 sentences) describing the ways you better understand cultures in your country specifically because of what you learned about their music.

PBL Website Project Guiding Question

How does traditional, popular, and national music of Africa reflect the values, experiences, and needs of the people who use it?

PBL Website Project Goals

1. Increase awareness of the ethnic diversity of sub-Saharan Africa
2. Increase awareness of the variety of musical sounds created in sub-Saharan Africa
3. Better understand how music is a form of human expression that is created in response to particular needs
4. Collaborate with other students in planning and creating an imagined website
5. Bring together the skills and knowledge of a small group with a united purpose

PBL Website Project Learning Outcomes

1. A view of modern Africa as comprised of countries that are each a unique combination of diverse ethnic groups with a variety of languages, customs, and musical traditions
2. An understanding of the sounds, settings, and significance of a few specific musical traditions practiced by particular ethnic groups living in the country under study
3. A greater awareness of the diversity of Africa's popular music, particularly as a response to the needs of modern Africans (Table 7.2)

Table 7.2 Website Assessment Rubric

Element	Target	Emerging	Needs Improvement
Site Plan	A plan that includes four examples for each student in the group. The plan includes appropriate distribution of ethnic groups and types of music, including traditional, popular, and the national anthem of each country.	The plan incorporates a variety of ethnic groups and styles that are not appropriately distributed or missing the national anthem of a country.	The plan contains little or no variety of ethnic groups and styles, or is missing input from group members.

For each of four examples per group member:

Element	Target	Emerging	Needs Improvement
Example	A musical example that is appropriate to the assignment, along with date recorded and performers.	A musical example appropriate to the assignment with unknown date and performers.	A musical example from the wrong country or not of the ethnic group ascribed by the student.
Blurb Accuracy	Complete accuracy of facts, names, and description of musical example, including link to online media.	Mostly accurate with some guesses or misspellings, and/or link missing.	Information missing or inaccurate.
Blurb Originality/ Style	Written in the student's own words, in a manner that effectively conveys the information.	Mostly original text with some use of cut and pasted phrases or some confusing language.	Overuse of cut and pasted phrases and/or confusing language.
People	Accurate description of the ethnic group and age range utilizing this music.	Mostly complete description with some information missing or inaccurate.	Information regarding people who utilize this music missing or inaccurate.

(Continued)

Table 7.2 (Continued)

Element	Target	Emerging	Needs Improvement
Sound	Detailed description of instruments, musical texture, and style, using vocabulary introduced in the class (pattern, polyrhythm, improvisation, etc.).	Description of instruments, musical texture, and style that is not complete or contains inaccuracies.	Information missing or inaccurate.
Setting	Detailed description of where and when this music is used.	Description missing some key information or detail.	Information missing or inaccurate.
Significance	Detailed description of the significance this music holds for a specific imagined performer or listener.	Description of the significance of this music that lacks detail or does not refer to a specific imagined performer or listener.	Missing or incomplete.
Post website completion:			
Intra-Group Feedback	At least four sentences containing detailed responses to each of four examples and blurbs completed by group members.	Four responses that are incomplete or lack detail.	Fewer than four responses.
Reflection	Complete and detailed answers to four reflection questions.	Answers to reflection questions that are incomplete or lack detail.	Fewer than four answers.

Outcomes

Student contributions to their group websites reflected a wide range of assignment completeness and accuracy. These four sample blurbs (incidentally, not written by music majors) represent writing that fulfills the requirements of the assignment.

Selected Sample of Student "Blurbs"

Below are four examples of student's work. Each "blurb" was accompanied by a link to an online video or audio clip.

National Anthem of Ghana: "God Bless Our Homeland Ghana"

The person who wrote and composed the national anthem was Phillip Gbeho. It was pointed toward everyone who lived in Ghana. It was to symbolize their independence from the British people who colonized them. The instruments that were used were trumpets, horns, trombone, and tuba. They are in a brass quintet. The tuba and trombone are the lower instruments and are the bass parts of the song, while the trumpets and horns are the higher parts of the song and they carry out the melody and harmonic accompaniment to the melody. This song was created in Ghana and is listened to by all of the Ghanaians that are happy and proud that their country was able to gain their independence in 1957. The music means a lot to the people who perform and listen to it because they want to play the song as gracefully and as impacting as possible because this symbolizes a great day in Ghanaian history.

Traditional Music from Zambia: "Kamutonga"

Traditional Zambian music is used to heal, teach, and celebrate life. This music reflects Zambian culture. Everyone at these traditional functions is part of the music. Some people make music with their hands and mouths while other people dance, making music with their bodies. The people there dance to fully connect with their people from both the past and future. The Makishi Dance is extremely inclusive allowing everyone to sing, dance, and clap to honor the spirits. There are people in costumes who appeal to or become the spirits, and it is an insult to ask who is behind the mask. There are drums beating quickly, and the Zambian people are dancing as fast as the beats that are being played. These drums could be Ngomas which are generally used for healing ceremonies but can be used for other things. This song and dance are for the Luvale youth to learn traditional values.

Traditional Music from Chad: "Maba Music"

The Maba people are a minority group found in the Ouaddai region in eastern Chad. At an earlier point in time, it was a powerful kingdom that ruled a vast area. They speak a language called Bura Mabang but still have a strong connection to the Arabic language. The Maba people are known to be very conservative people with a strong sense of identity and the resistance to change. They have an estimated population of about 700,000. This music of the Maba people contains the chanting of a man and a woman, drumming and clapping. You can also note that there's a sort of marching sound with the clapping and the drums. This sounds like it could be some sort of traveling song preparing for battle.

Popular Music from Democratic Republic of the Congo: "Street Music"

This music is created by everyday people for the everyday citizen of the nation. It speaks for those stuck in poverty and in the ghettos. It sings words of hope and passed down wisdom to continue overcoming the obstacles life has set. The instruments are whatever they can find or make, true creativity and innovation. Out of all the genres, this was my favorite because it sounds true and gives you a real glimpse of what it is like to love out in their nation. The artists of these songs are singing to portray their struggle into words and a visual image while still managing to be happy. This music is the true epitome of happiness in the struggle.

Intra-Group Student Feedback (Assignment Step 3)

Intra-group feedback by students provided evidence of connections they made to the music via this assignment, here categorized into three types with illustrative student quotes:

1. **Connections to existing knowledge and experience**
   "This man … reminds me of Jamaican reggae artist Bulu Banton."
   "It's mixed with hip-hop and gospel flow."
   "This song reminds me of a song that is popular and played a lot at parties today, called Tekno -Pana."
   "I like this example of *seggae*, because reggae is one of my favorite genres."
   "This music reminds me of American pop and hip-hop music because of the type of instruments they use … [and] the beats are similar."
   "This [Ugandan dancehall] reminds me a lot of Jamaican dancehall because of the way it's danced."

2. **Connections to knowledge and experiences gained in this class**
   "I like how you gave some insight [in]to the lyrics of the song and how you connected it to colonialism."
   "This song sounds similar to my country's song of independence."

"I like this example because this song is one of the reasons Ewe people became respected for their sophistication."

"The South African national anthem reflects the multinational nature of the country. The anthem conveys the struggle the South African people went through for freedom."

"This music reminds me of an ethnic group in Ghana because of the shakers."

3. **Curiosity for new experiences and connections**
"I would like to know more about the oldest instrument in Sudan that she mentioned."

"It's interesting to see how music worldwide is similar even though we might think otherwise because of language differences."

"I want to know more about the types of wars that took place that caused this war song to be produced."

"I would like to know more about what [this] ceremony is for and what it means to the community."

"I would like to know more about Kouyate's background and how his past influences
the music he performs."

"I was able to play it repeatedly. Great music choice."

Written Reflection (Assignment Step 4)

Students wrote reflections giving insight into what they took from the process and content of this assignment. A few themes emerged. Almost every student mentioned the ethnic diversity in Africa and its manifestation in musical creation and use as being an important part of what they learned. Many spoke of the difficulties they encountered trying to find accurate information regarding the musical examples they chose. When asked to "describe the ways you better understand cultures in your country specifically because of what you learned about their music," students responded with empathy and a sense of discovery, as illustrated in these excerpts:

"I understand their love and compassion through the music they make."

"Music is a way of discovering new cultures and provides an aural platform to see how people live their lives, what they like and don't like, and how they spend their time."

"By listening to their music and seeing the culture through their eyes and not from the media, I have a better understanding of what they are as a people and country."

"Different types of songs were used to support the community in different ways – whether it was a farming song, warrior song, *djeli* song, etc. I find that music is used differently there, and I think that's one of the things I enjoyed the most about this class."

Assessment

It has been my experience that students tend not to like group projects. They find them unnecessarily complicated with the extra layer of finding times and means of collaborating. In this instance as well, students showed resistance when I presented the assignment. Once immersed in the project, however, most students exhibited a greater sense of class cohesion and respect for one another. As one student wrote regarding the group aspect in her reflection, "it went better than expected, quick and easy messages passed on to one another and splitting the work or at least having someone encouraging and pushing towards a certain direction to complete the assignment helps."

I identified three concrete markers of success, which are demonstrated in the student writing samples above. First, the musical examples and blurbs themselves showed that students carefully considered what should be included in a representative website for their country. Second, the comments students made about their group members' work showed that they were making connections outside of their direct research and writing. Third, the types of learning that they reported in their final reflection showed a depth of understanding and appreciation that I had not experienced in past versions of the "Your Country" assignment.

As with any endeavor, and particularly with the first use of a new strategy, there were moments of failure. One student absolutely refused to participate in the group aspect of this assignment and would only complete the separate tasks on his own. Some students sent each other the material late or incomplete, making it difficult for the entire group to turn things in on time. Some students misread the assignment and turned in the wrong types of material, requiring group members to spend extra time setting them straight. These were minor problems compared to the benefits of using PBL. I am already planning to implement an expanded and revised version of this project when I teach MUS 209 in J-Term 2018.

In the future, I will use PBL for the entire series of "Your Country" assignments. I found that when students had to decide what information was important and necessary, they fully engaged in the process, so that while they memorized and regurgitated fewer pieces of information, they connected more deeply to what they learned. I also plan to implement a similar project in my MUS 208 Survey of World Music Cultures course.

Bibliography

Khapoya, Vincent B. *The African Experience, Fourth Edition*. Upper Saddle River, NJ: Pearson, 2013.

Savery, John R. "Overview of Problem-based Learning: Definitions and Distinctions." *Interdisciplinary Journal of Problem-based Learning* 1/I, 2006, 9–20.

Shelemay, Kay Kaufman. *Soundscapes: Exploring Music in a Changing World, Third Edition*. New York: W.W. Norton, 2015.

8

Designing and Implementing Collaborative Student-Driven Research Projects: A New Framework for Learning in the Ethnomusicology Classroom

JULIE E. HUNTER

In this final chapter concerning ethnomusicology, Julie implements three different Problem-based Learnings in two courses – two in an upper-division African Music course and one in a lower-division World Music Cultures class. The two courses could not be more different, and the results of a PBL "in your own backyard," so to speak, versus a PBL on a culture half a world away could not be more enlightening. Julie's experiences with the three PBLs give great insight into the group learning process, as she shares some of the challenges of group work and how she overcame them.

Funtumfunafu ne dɛnkyɛmfunafu, wɔn afuru bom nanso woredidi a na wɔreko

efiri sɛ aduane dɛ yɛte no wɔ menetwitwie mu.[1]

—Akan proverb about the importance of cooperation,
and the strength of unity in diversity

~

In 2015, I met with music colleagues from across the State University of New York (SUNY) system on the exploration and implementation of Problem-based Learning (PBL) practices in our courses, which introduced me to the teaching approach of PBL. Since that time, I have incorporated PBL projects into three courses at the Crane School of Music at SUNY Potsdam where I serve as Assistant Professor of Ethnomusicology. This chapter explores this exciting new approach by applying PBL methodology to an ethnomusicology course.

Reflections on Teaching Ethnomusicology

Over the course of my years as an educator, I have often embraced new approaches to learning and teaching. As a Ph.D. student in ethnomusicology at

Brown University during the 2000s, I was introduced to the innovative idea of a flexible and student-centered curriculum – a hallmark of Brown's educational system. One significant aspect of Brown's curriculum is the option for students to create their own major. The Crane School of Music, where I currently work, is a teaching-focused university with a long history of emphasizing high-quality music education and a student-driven curriculum. The Music Education program has the largest number of music majors in Crane and attracts the most music students to campus each year. Crane students tend to be leaders in the classroom. In addition, they often direct major events, serve on committees, including faculty committees, and shape the curriculum and programs in unique ways, giving them a strong voice at the university. Given this environment, I have spent much of my time here exploring the intersections of teaching and scholarship, and searching for ways to improve and transform my teaching. For example, I developed innovative approaches to West African music performance as the director of the Crane West African Drum and Dance Ensemble.

These experiences have greatly influenced my perspective on student learning, and I have frequently adopted teaching strategies that emphasize a high level of student involvement, leadership, and negotiation. Such strategies include student discussion leading, input on syllabi, peer evaluation and feedback, and presentation of student research projects in the classroom and at professional events. The ideas and methods utilized in PBL, therefore, were an extension of these pedagogical strategies, which have greatly impacted my general perspective on teaching in all of my courses.

While the existing ethnomusicological scholarship provides numerous texts and resources for the pedagogy of world music,[2] there has been limited focus on specific methodologies for innovative teaching strategies that can apply to various types of courses. I have noted that there is a limited focus on a "pedagogy of ethnomusicology," especially beyond the framework of a world music course or ethnomusicology ensemble. In addition, few ethnomusicology graduate courses are solely devoted to teaching students about how to design, approach, and implement an ethnomusicology course.[3] The primary types of creative and applied learning projects which are provided as a model for ethnomusicology courses are usually focused on doing fieldwork and creating ethnographies. While this is an extremely valuable experience, especially for students moving into ethnomusicology graduate programs, there is much room for discussion on the potential benefits of other types of student projects, including PBL projects, and how to implement them.

Overview on Problem-Based Learning in Higher Education

As I thought about ways of implementing PBL, I realized that the PBL framework can be incorporated through both ongoing day-to-day modes of inquiry and interaction in the classroom, as well as larger-scale research projects that span the semester. According to John Savery, PBL was first introduced in the context of medical education in order for doctors to most effectively diagnose patients (9–10). Savery explains that the medical program at McMaster University in Canada first piloted this approach (10). Medical students frequently practice hypothetical deductive reasoning in order to prepare for exams and real-life situations. Numerous studies point to the fact that medical students who trained with the PBL model not only performed just as well on exams as those using traditional models but "exhibited better clinical problem-solving skills" (Savery, 10). While PBL has commonly been used in medical education in North America since the 1980s, it is much less common within today's undergraduate curriculum. As Natalie Sarrazin observes in Chapter 1, few music instructors in higher education have published on this topic, with Hon-Lun Yang's article in the *Journal of Music History Pedagogy* providing one of the few examples of PBL in the college music classroom.

By adopting a PBL approach, I have been able to guide students in projects that highlight the use of creative resources and tools, 21st-century technologies, and collaboration and interaction in the learning process. By grappling with a PBL question, which typically does not have a single answer, students are faced with the need to apply the knowledge they have learned in a unique, creative, or socially relevant manner. David Jonassen and Woei Hung explain that in PBL "knowledge building is stimulated by the problem and applied back to the problem" (2012: 2687). Rather than simply introducing content, and designing research around a given topic or prescribed final project, many teachers adopting PBL emphasize the open-ended and student-driven learning that can unfold. This method encourages students to develop and practice skills that are essential in the 21st century, and across disciplines and career paths. These projects can also result in unexpected and original contributions from students to the field of ethnomusicology.

PBL Project Design and Descriptions

In the fall of both 2015 and 2017, I developed PBL projects in Music, Culture and Politics in West Africa (MUCH 395), and in the spring of 2016, I incorporated a PBL project into World Music Cultures (MUCH 360). Both of these courses are upper-division electives for music majors, though Arts and Science students can register with permission. Both count toward the Africana Studies minor. While I teach courses oriented toward music and nonmusic majors each semester, it seemed as though majors would be particularly excited about engaging in the PBL process. Students could potentially draw on the techniques and experience of PBL in their future careers in fields such as Music Education, Performance, Business, Composition, and Musicology. In addition, the project seemed best suited to an upper-division class given its more extensive nature. Within each class, the overarching questions posed were different; however, there was consistency established between the projects, which allowed for comparison. The similarities between the PBL projects included length of time of implementation, size of groups, types of project activities, overall weight within the breakdown of grades, and application of peer collaboration and feedback.

I first designed and taught Music, Culture, and Politics in West Africa at Crane in 2014. The course centers on traditional and popular music in West Africa and its significance in both historical and contemporary perspective. Genres studied include *highlife*, *juju*, *afrobeat*, *mbalax*, and traditional Mande, Tuareg, Wolof, Ga, Akan, Vai, and Yoruba styles. Topics covered consist of talking drums, organology, concepts of rhythm, European musical influences, colonial and postcolonial politics, gender roles, music and religion, music and nationalism, music and conflict, modes of transmission, and the history and analysis of repertoire. The major goals of the course are for students to become familiar with contemporary cultures of the region and the political and social dimensions of music making, increase their listening and analytical skills, and further their communication skills via in-class presentations, discussions, and projects. In addition to the PBL project, other requirements encompass reading, web assignments, discussion leading, listening journals, listening-based quizzes, and a song performance project (Table 8.1).

The research question posed for Project 1 in the fall of 2015 was *"how would you design an engaging cultural experience in West Africa for your colleagues?"* The main objective of this project was for students to explore music and culture in one region of West Africa in greater depth and creatively apply this knowledge to design a representative cultural experience for that region highlighted through text, multimedia, visual, and/or performance modes. While the project format was open-ended, as discussed below, there were specific components required from each group comprised of 2–3 students. For the same course in the fall of 2017, the Project 3 question was different – *"how can you make Ewe music meaningful to 21ˢᵗ Century audiences?"*[4] The objective of this project was for students to investigate one issue in or aspect of Ewe

Table 8.1 PBL Questions

Project 1: Music, Culture, and Politics in West Africa	How would you design an engaging cultural experience in West Africa for your colleagues?
Project 2: World Music Cultures	Where is traditional music in the North Country?
Project 3: Music, Culture, and Politics in West Africa	How can you make Ewe music meaningful to 21st-century audiences?

music and apply the information learned to the research problem by making it meaningful in some way to contemporary audiences. For this project, there was a single group of four students.

In the spring of 2016, I utilized PBL in World Music Cultures, implementing Project 2. In this course, students consider music as a human phenomenon and look at how people make music in various parts of the contemporary world, including how people organize music, what the sounds mean and signify to them, and how music embodies and reflects the cultures and places from which it comes. They examine music in selected regions of North America, Latin America and the Caribbean, Africa, and Asia. Topics covered typically include Navajo music and ritual, the blues, Cuban hip hop and politics, Ewe drumming and dancing, Dominican *Merengue* and nationalism, Javanese *gamelan*, and film music in India. The major goals of this course are for students to further their musical listening skills across a broad range of genres and styles, increase their ability to write clearly about music, and expand their knowledge and critical understanding of peoples' cultures and histories in several regions of the world. Other requirements include reading, quizzes, listening-based exams, web assignments, and listening journals. Students in this class addressed the question *"where is traditional music in the North Country?"* I designed a research problem that allowed students to connect with their backgrounds and experiences as many grew up in New York State, including North Country communities in Upstate New York. The open-ended nature of this project and students' proximity to the region enabled them to adopt field-work methods and actively engage with music in the local community, if they chose to. There were four groups of three students in the class.

By taking these courses, it is hoped that students will expand their understanding of music beyond the Western canon and gain a foundation for teaching and performing global music. One major goal is to raise students' awareness of issues of diversity, social justice, and music in the context of communities. PBL provides an important methodology to address these broader ethnomusicological goals by enabling students to engage with authentic, real-life experiences and situations.

Process of Implementation

I introduced the research project early in the semester at which time the students were given their research problem, required components, and guidelines for completion. The research components included group notes, an annotated bibliography, in-class presentation, final project, and individual reflective essay. The due dates were established at set intervals for the project's components. The ongoing submissions reflected each group's research process throughout the semester and enabled for continual feedback. Presentations took place during the final week of the semester. The final projects were then due the following week during the exam period. Several days after turning in the final project, students were asked to hand in a reflection on their experience (see the Appendix).

In addition to handouts with the project guidelines and due dates, I created drop boxes on the course Moodle (the college's teaching website platform) site for each of the submissions. Each of the drop boxes was placed in chronological order of due date under the assignment section at the top of the site and included more detailed information for each post. The due dates also appeared in the online course calendar. Links to potential useful resources, such as the Afropop Worldwide, Smithsonian Folkways, and Traditional Arts of Upstate New York (TAUNY) websites, were posted under the course resources section on the Moodle site. As students began to brainstorm and clarify the focus of their projects, I took photographs of in-class notes and posted them for reference on Moodle. This helped to ensure that all would have access to the information and feel included in the process.

While students were aware of the research project from the start of the semester, we did not begin to select groups and brainstorm on topics, until four weeks into the semester. The group selection process varied by class. Students selected their own groups for Projects 1 and 3, while in Project 2, students were assigned to a group. Groups were encouraged to select several topics of interest to them during an in-class meeting and continue conversation around those topics outside of class in order to hone in on a topic that would be appealing to all. Once groups and topics were in place, students also shared information about their individual performance, creative, research, and technological strengths. This encouraged students to identify the skills and roles that each member could contribute. In order for groups to meet and share their progress, class time was designated throughout the semester. This enabled students to receive vital feedback and locate additional resources. While I provided suggestions on the general content and feasibility of projects, I tried to avoid being overly directive about suggestions for the project format, design, resources, and ways to accomplish their goals. The process of discovery, and identification of tools and resources by students, is emphasized as part of the PBL approach (see Sarrazin in Chapter 1).

The projects culminated in group presentations at the end of the semester. The presentations lasted between 20 and 25 minutes per group with an opportunity for comments and questions at the end. Following presentations, peer-feedback forms were provided for each student (see the Appendix). This was extremely valuable as groups received suggestions for making improvements which they could use to finish or edit their projects before the final submission a week later. To close out the project, students each submitted individual reflections on their experience and the contributions of group members.

Case Studies of Student Work

By examining numerous case studies from all three of these courses, I was able to gain a deeper understanding of the value of PBL in several contexts. For Project 1 in Music, Culture, and Politics in West Africa, "*how would you design an engaging cultural experience in West Africa?*", the final projects included topics on The Festival in the Desert, Music Education in Ghana, and Music and Urban Culture in Accra. For the first project in this list, students created a poster and PowerPoint on a cultural experience designed around the Festival in the Desert, an international music festival based in the Northern Malian town of Timbuktu. They provided information about the history of the festival, the politics surrounding the strife in northern Mali which led to the festival's recent closure, specific artists who have played a vital role in the festival, and an analysis of songs by these artists. They also included details about the nature of their proposed cultural experience such as cost, lodging, and planned cultural sites. Their project clearly addressed a potential study abroad experience around the PBL problem by creating an itinerary of destinations in Mali and outlining information on the specifics of their designed trip.

For the second project in this class, students explored music education in Ghana. They created a ten-minute documentary video about music institutions such as music education in the history and context of the University of Ghana, Legon, and the Achimota School. They offered a brief background on Ghana and history of each institution, including key figures related to their history and connection to the cultural politics at the time of establishment, and discussion of the types of musics taught. They also made the topic meaningful by addressing how their colleagues at the Crane School of Music would benefit from this type of cultural experience. Their presentation consisted of a short introduction to, and a screening of, the video.

The final group designed a six-panel brochure on music and urban culture in Accra with images, text, and scholarly quotes. On their brochure, they featured several QR codes with links to a radio show, music videos, and further reading which included a bibliography of key sources for their project. They also created a highly engaging and well-researched PowerPoint which elaborated on key issues and examples from the brochure. They offered background on music and culture in Accra, leading popular *hiplife* artists, key urban performance sites, such as the Chale Wote Street Art Festival, and unique social issues addressed by contemporary artists (Figure 8.1).

In contrast, for Project 2 in World Music Cultures, project topics included "An Academic Approach to the Music of La Bottine Souriante,"[5] "My Adirondack Home," and "Music of the North Country: How Crane Has Made an Impact on Northern New York." In response to the question about locating traditional music in the North Country, one group created a website for their project titled "My Adirondack Home." This website highlighted music

Additional Resources:

FOKN Bois Interview:

Afropop Worldwide

> Program: Hip Deep Ghana 2
> From Gospel to Hiplife

Further
Reading:

Bike Lordz
Video:

**MUSIC AND
POPULAR CULTURE**

Accra, the capital city of Ghana,
has a wide variety of music from its
traditional music of the Ga & Ewe,
as well as the musics of the Akan
percussion ensembles through
Adowa & Kete. Some of Accra's
popular forms of music are Highlife
Kpanlogo, Afro-beat, Gospel, and
Hiplife. Along with the wide range of
music, Accra has become a cultural
metropolitan area. "It is the largest
growing city in Ghana with a
population of over 26 million
people as of 2015." Accra houses
a wide range of artists in areas like
Jamestown by highlighting them in
monthly festivals and galleries but
also on the streets of Accra. At
Labadi beach there is a weekly
performance of local musicians
especially those who focus on
Ghanaian Reggae music, but if you
are more into the history side of
Accra you can visit the W.E.B.
Dubois Cultural Center as well
Kwame Nkruman Mausoleum
Memorial Park. All throughout
Accra you can see areas that have
been influenced from pre, post,
and colonial Ghana which shows
Ghana's wide range of culture.

**MUSIC AND
URBAN
CULTURE**
OF ACCRA, GHANA

Narise Connor, Brandon Griffin,
& Chelsea Frirsz Hillerich

Because of negative stereotyping
and the state of her economies,
Africa is often viewed as a third-
world continent. Many people
unfairly associate Africa with
impressions of barren plains and
feral animals. However, what
many fail to realize is that Africa is
home to bustling cities that
contain unique and colorful urban
cultures. As the largest city in
Ghana - Accra is an important
cultural center that represents
modern urban living in Africa.

Figure 8.1 Three panels of a six-panel brochure on popular music and culture in
Accra created by students in Music, Culture, and Politics in West Africa

in the North Country with an introduction on the homepage and separate
pages devoted to "Local Musicians," "Upcoming Concerts," "Interview," and
"Sources." On the homepage, the group posted a video of their creative interpretation and performance of the folk song "My Adirondack Home." According to Dave Ruch, the producer of the *Songs to Keep* recording project,
this song was performed by Francis DeLong on February 4, 1951 and documented by North Country folk song collector Marjorie Lansing Porter using
a Soundscriber recorder. The *Songs to Keep* project was organized by the Traditional Arts of Upstate New York (TAUNY) in 2013, and it featured an audio
recording of contemporary artists performing songs from Porter's collection,
a documentary film directed by Paul Larson, and a 40-page songbook. The
Bacon Brothers (a duo consisting of brothers Michael Bacon and Kevin, the
award-winning actor) recorded a version of "My Adirondack Home" featured
on the recording and film. The students' video highlights their rendition of
the song – arranged for voice, guitar, and flute – which was modeled after the
Bacon Brothers' recording and includes beautifully shot footage of this scenic
region (Figure 8.2).

For Project 3, students responded to the question "*how can you make Ewe
music meaningful for 21st Century audiences?*" by creating a project highlighting Ewe women's music. They believed that it was important to acknowledge

We also created a cover of the folk song "My Adirondack Home", which was originally recorded by Marjorie Lansing Porter, a woman who dedicated years of her life recording folk songs in the Adirondacks in the early 1900s. It was recently re-recorded by the Bacon Brothers for the film *Songs to Keep*. Our music video was all filmed around our Adirondack home, Potsdam, NY.

Figure 8.2 An image from the homepage of a student project on music in the North Country, including their video of the folk song "My Adirondack Home"

Ewe women's underrepresented music making. They designed a PowerPoint with information about gender in Ewe culture, musical gender roles, instrumentation, gendered musical aesthetics, and primarily female-oriented dance-drumming genres such as *bobo*, *husago*, and *bobobo* (see Burns 2009; Hunter 2012; Younge 2011). In addition, it was exciting that they drew on information from my dissertation entitled "The Rise of Women's Drumming in Africa: Performing Gender and Transforming Community in Southeastern Ghana." While the group explored and summarized important content on the topic, they could have engaged with the research question more thoroughly. In order to make the material socially relevant, they interviewed a colleague at SUNY Potsdam in an effort not only to share information they had learned but survey their colleague's knowledge on and response to the topic. They had hoped that this portion of the project would have been more extensive.

PBL Assessment

Projects were assessed based on groups' response to the research problem, feasibility of design, depth of information, breadth and validity of sources, clarity and organization of ideas, creativity, and critical thinking. They were also assessed on their collaborative interaction and individual investment. Each group received a grade for their completed project. Points were awarded for each aspect of this rubric, though the specific breakdown of points varied by class. Individual group members received a separate grade determined by their personal contributions as evidenced by their in-class group participation and reflective essays. While the smaller project components, such as the annotated bibliography and group notes, were not actually given a grade, points were deducted at the end for missing or late work.

In addition to instructor assessment, I incorporated peer assessment into the projects. As mentioned earlier, at the end of the semester, students evaluated each other's projects and presentations by way of peer-feedback forms. They answered questions about presentations, including the effectiveness of the organization of presentations, interaction of groups, professionalism, and clarity and communication of ideas. There was a place to write general comments and make at least one constructive suggestion. Everyone, including the instructor, gave the anonymous forms to each group at the end of class.

While I provided the general assessment rubric above in the project guidelines, in retrospect it might have been beneficial to create a more detailed grading rubric and share it with students early in the semester. This would help to convey the expectations and highlight the desired competencies emphasized by the PBL project (see, for example, Tracy Wanamaker's detailed grading rubric in Chapter 12).

Reflection on PBL Process

Overall, the students responded well to the project. It appears that the project timeline, structure, assignments, peer feedback, and assessments were generally successful and effective. Many students expressed an initial enthusiasm about the project at the start of the semester. The excitement seemed to continue as they worked as a team and moved from the brainstorming phase, to determining a topic and format, and figuring out ways to meet their goals. There appeared to be a feeling of excitement in the classroom when we shifted gears on the days when students discussed their research activities and they took on active leadership and discussion roles. They shared ideas, guided each other, and engaged in an intricate process of negotiation. It was very rewarding for all to see the final results. In addition, I believe that the experience enhanced students' level of engagement and energy in the course during the semester.

While the PBL experience was generally successful and well received by students, a number of challenges emerged in all three classes. During Project 1, tension developed as students made final decisions regarding group member selection. There were eight students in the class. Four students were interested in the same topic, but the groups would have been less balanced in terms of numbers. I stepped in and made the final decision which I did not expect to do. Throughout the semester, one of the groups worked effectively and efficiently without fail. They maintained focus and turned in all assignments on time. Another group modified their topic, and fell behind, but came out in the end with a successful project. The third group appeared to be less organized, and members reflected in their essays that they could have devoted more time to their research activities, but their project was still engaging and informative.

Based on the extensive time spent to select groups for Project 1, I decided to select groups randomly for Project 2 in World Music Cultures. Issues still arose with group selection as many students reflected at the end of the semester that they could have worked better with their friends given scheduling conflicts. For Project 3, therefore, students had the option to choose their own groups. Given the small size of the class, they could create two groups of two or one of four people. They chose to work as one group. As a result of this experience, it appears that it is most effective for there to be at least two groups working simultaneously on projects in one class while still providing impetus and feedback to each other. In addition, while group size and the number of groups per class can certainly vary, as Sarrazin points out in Chapter 1, smaller groups of 2–4 students seem to work best.

From my experience and observation, it appears that the major issue students faced is how to communicate and collaborate effectively, and reach a consensus on how to bring the project to fruition. In some cases, they felt concern and hesitation toward participating in group work, in part because of negative past experiences with group projects, especially in high school. Some may hold the preconceived notion that group learning is "a waste of time." Others may be concerned that their grade could be negatively affected by the work of their peers. Based on this feedback, in future semesters, I will discuss guidelines for effective communication and group interaction before the groups are formed, hopefully enabling a smoother start to the initial process of collaborating. I will also turn to existing scholarship in the field of education to learn additional strategies for facilitating effective group work and provide ideas for students on ways to successfully participate in groups (see Brame and Biel 2015; Johnson and Johnson 1999). As mentioned above, I would also recommend that groups begin to meet earlier in the semester. While some groups manage to complete their projects successfully in the last two months of the semester, others needed more time.

Other group challenges included missed deadlines and work being submitted at the last minute. One reason for this may be the difficulty in finding convenient meeting times. One solution might involve creating chat groups on Facebook, or meeting virtually over Skype or Google Hangouts. Several groups chose to use these platforms. Another issue that emerged, as students reflected in their essays, was that the work was not equally shared by all. In order to facilitate greater individual accountability and group equity, it might be helpful for students to engage in ongoing individual reflection on their role, and the interactions and work of the group. This could be factored into their class participation grade.

Another issue that emerged concerned student focus. In negotiating with students through the process, I found that students benefit from continual refocusing to ensure they maximize their time and do not diverge on too many tangents. In an effort to encourage students to maintain a clear focus and work more smoothly together, it might be helpful for them to undertake ongoing reflection on the purpose and goal of their project. As we discussed in the PBL workshop at SUNY Brockport, the instructor's advice should not significantly direct the project but gently guide it along the way. In some cases, I ended up giving more feedback than I would have liked, especially when it was clear students were struggling to narrow a topic, finalize the project format, and identify resources.

The project presentation also requires a thoughtful balance of research and information. For some groups, it was a challenge to locate and draw from the most valid and informative sources, while in other cases, the students became more concerned with the creative element. It is important for them to be grounded in the research content and PBL question, and not just focused on the creative side of the work. Students may have an inclination to rely primarily or solely on online sources. For that reason, I required an annotated bibliography with at least eight sources. Some students may find it difficult to thoroughly address a PBL question. Although I dedicated time during the semester for students to meet and work on the project, I would like to further integrate PBL into the syllabus. I feel that it would be extremely beneficial for students to read a short essay on PBL or explore a PBL website, such as "What Is Project Based Learning?", in order to acquire a deeper understanding of the research process and its value.

Given that PBL is student-driven, the instructor must be open to the direction of the conversations and ideas generated by the students. Since the process of learning and its research outcomes are so vastly different from one semester to the next, PBL provides a unique experience for the instructor as well. While this can create a level of excitement and surprise for instructors, it also poses challenges in how to most effectively guide projects. It appears to work best when instructors are flexible with the course schedule, and willing to sacrifice covering content on the syllabus if necessary. Although we spent about 3–4 classes on PBL projects, including presentations, this time was not always planned in advance. For example, during Project 3, we unexpectedly devoted an entire class for group discussion given that the student's progress was slower than anticipated. I also integrated an impromptu lecture on Ewe music near the end of the semester to establish background on the topic given that Ewe music is not studied extensively within the course. It is important to spend class time when necessary to enable in-class group work, and provide this focused feedback to each group.

In general, I had some moments of concern within each course given that the research process was so transparent. However, I believe that the transparency of the research process, and instructor's guidance of the group work, is what makes this method so effective. Instructors utilizing PBL can be involved in students' research throughout the semester, thus embedding the PBL directly into the classroom experience. This provides an important level of support that is not always as prominent or significant in the structure of more traditional academic teaching. By being accountable to their group, students tend to be less likely to wait until the last minute to work on a project. Another major benefit is that the process of research is not only collaborative, transparent, and encourages feedback, but it can also enable students to experience the process of knowledge production and how it may vary from one individual or group to the next. This allows students to gain a level of reflexivity about researching and the research process that may not be possible otherwise. Thus, through PBL, there is an epistemological lens in which students are encouraged to reflect on how it is that they know what they know through documenting and evaluating the research process. Therefore, students take away more than new information, resources, and skills; they gain a deeper understanding of how knowledge is produced by various individuals, and the value of knowledge production.

Implications for PBL in Ethnomusicology

PBL is an innovative teaching method with great potential for student learning in the ethnomusicology classroom. I plan to continue to incorporate PBL projects and teaching strategies into my courses in the future. While there are challenges to overcome, as I discuss above, I am convinced of the value of this method, especially for undergraduate music majors. As noted earlier, this initiative and book importantly contribute to the limited practice and scholarship on PBL in the higher education music classroom. Since being introduced to PBL, I have utilized many more active, student-centered, and question-driven strategies than in the past. PBL has the potential not only to make course material more meaningful and relevant but enhance students' skills in problem-solving, critical thinking, creativity, interdisciplinary approaches, and interactive learning.

While PBL can prompt students to sharpen their skills in analyzing, evaluating, understanding, and remembering content, it can also importantly facilitate opportunities for higher-level thinking, such as creating and applying (see Bloom's Taxonomy). Instructors also simultaneously learn from their students, much more so than in a typical research project with a directed format. For example, through this process, students can introduce instructors to current resources including innovative 21st-century technologies. It can allow for students to become the expert, and there is value in encouraging students to create original ideas and contributions that could be drawn on by others. Although the collaborative nature of this student-driven learning can be challenging for both students and instructor, from my work as an ethnomusicologist, I can easily see the benefit of problem-solving and collaborating in a group setting for a class project. Ethnomusicologists frequently work closely with others and collaborate as part of the paradigms of both doing fieldwork and performing (see Titon 2008 and Beaudry 2008).

Many proponents of PBL argue that the collaborative experience is one of the most significant benefits, especially given that most 21st-century jobs require collaborative skills. While music majors need to employ collaborative skills in the context of performance, these do not easily translate into a collaborative research setting. How can one transfer the creativity, energy, and collaboration of performing in a group to the process of researching within a group? Music Educators Caron Collins and Danni Gilbert explore 21st-century approaches to teaching ensembles and draw on the flipped classroom model in their e-book titled *Curious, Collaborative Creativity: A Guide for Transforming Music Ensembles* (2017). They focus on the important role of student collaboration and leadership. While their teaching strategies and materials are centered around music ensembles, many of these ideas and resources could be applied to ethnomusicology courses and provide an innovative approach to guiding group work and collaboration in the undergraduate music classroom.

As ethnomusicologists could benefit from more collaborative research activity at all levels of study and work, PBL could provide a model for collaborative ethnomusicological research. Furthermore, given the larger teaching goals of ethnomusicologists to increase students' awareness of diversity, equity, social justice, and diverse ways of being musical and experiencing music in the world, PBL can provide a framework for introducing students to important issues and concepts in an engaging and socially relevant way while also encouraging and extending conversations on these topics across disciplines, programs, and within, and outside of, the academy.

Appendix

Tables A8.1 and A8.2

Table A8.1 Overview of PBL Process

1. Select Topic	Post initial topic/format on Moodle discussion board
2. Written Submission #1	Submit all group notes on Moodle drop box
3. Written Submission #2	Submit all group notes since Written Submission #1 on Moodle drop box
4. Annotated Bibliography	Submit an annotated bibliography of at least 8 sources on Moodle drop box
5. In-Class Presentation	Present research during 20–25 minutes group presentation, followed by peer feedback
6. Final Project	Submit final project, including any new group notes, and supplemental material
7. Individual Reflection	Submit 3–4 pages reflection based on experience on Moodle drop box

Table A8.2 PBL Peer-Feedback Form

Please circle the most appropriate response for the following questions and provide some comments and suggestions for your colleagues to use as they finish their project, and prepare for future presentations.

1. The presentation was well organized in terms of the structure of the content, order of topics and information, and involvement of group participants.
    a) Very well organized
    b) Organized relatively well
    c) Could use improvement in organization
    d) Difficult to follow based on organization

2. The specific topic of the project chosen by this group is appropriate to the research question posed.
    a) Strongly agree
    b) Agree
    c) Agree somewhat
    d) Disagree

3. The project, and its final format, is intriguing, engaging, and targeted toward you and your colleagues.
    a) Strongly agree
    b) Agree
    c) Agree somewhat
    d) Disagree

(Continued)

Table A8.2 (Continued)

4. The presentation was aided by helpful learning devices such as powerPoint, video and audio clips, and/or handouts.
    a) Strong learning aids
    b) Good learning aids
    c) Limited learning aids
    d) Difficult to follow in relation to clarity of ideas and/or no learning aids

5. The presentation group chose solid examples to highlight their project, such as music, video clips, and/or cultural information, and these examples were used in an effective way.
    a) Excellent selection of examples
    b) Good selection of examples
    c) Fair selection of examples
    d) Could have chosen better examples

6. The presentation group actively engaged the class throughout the session, and effectively responded to questions.
    a) Excellent engagement of class
    b) Good engagement of class
    c) Fair engagement of class
    d) Engagement of class could use work; little interaction

7. The presenters showed enthusiasm for the topic/project.
    a) Very enthusiastic
    b) Relatively enthusiastic
    c) Could use more enthusiasm
    d) Little evidence of enthusiasm

8. The presenters appeared professional in relation to posture, stance, movement, and interaction with one another.
    a) Appeared highly professional
    b) Appeared professional
    c) Appeared somewhat professional
    d) Could use improvement in posture, stance, eye contact, etc.

9. Please make one suggestion for the group which they may be able to incorporate into their final PBL project. This could include something that you found somewhat confusing, an idea or issue that needs further research, a point which they did not have a chance to address, and/or an aspect of the creative side of the project which could be improved in some way.

Notes

1 This Akan proverb from Ghana describes two conjoined crocodiles, *funtumfunafu and dɛnkyemfunafu*, who share the same stomach, but when they are eating, they still fight over food because of its "sweetness" and taste. See "The Fifty Most Important Akan Proverbs."
2 See, for example, Titon (2017), Nettl and Rommen (2017), Shelemay (2015), and Campbell (2004).

3 One exception to this is ethnomusicologist Kiri Miller's course titled *Ethnomusicology Workshop* (MUSC 2085) at Brown University which provides an excellent overview for graduate students on how to effectively create and teach a course, and addresses a needed emphasis on pedagogy.
4 While this research question appears to be narrower in focus than in the previous classes, in this case, I developed the question during the course of the semester in response to student interest and feedback.
5 La Bottine Souriante is a French Canadian roots music band based in Quebec.

References

Adinkra Symbols: African Symbols from the Akans of Ghana. "The 50 Most Important Akan Proverbs". Accessed January 4, 2018. www.adinkrasymbols.org/the-50-most-important-akan-proverbs/.

Afropop Worldwide. Accessed January 19, 2018. http://afropop.org/.

Beaudry, Nicole. "The Challenges of Human Relations in Ethnographic Inquiry: Examples from Arctic and Subarctic Fieldwork". In *Shadows in the Field: New Perspectives for Fieldwork in Ethnomusicology*, edited by Gregory Barz and Timothy Cooley, 224–45. 2nd Edition. New York: Oxford University Press, 2008.

Brame, Cynthia J. and Rachel Biel. "Setting Up and Facilitating Group Work: Using Cooperative Learning Groups Effectively". 2015. Accessed January 3, 2018. http://cft.vanderbilt.edu/guides-sub-pages/setting-up-and-facilitating-group-work-using-cooperative-learning-groups-effectively/.

Burns, James. *Female Voices from an Ewe Dance-Drumming Community in Ghana: Our Music Has Become a Divine Spirit*. Burlington, VT: Ashgate, 2009.

Campbell, Patricia Shehan. *Teaching Music Globally*. New York: Oxford University Press, 2004.

Collins, Caron L. and Danni Gilbert. *Curious, Collaborative Creativity: A Guide for Transforming Music Ensembles*. E-book, 2017. www.curiouscollaborativecreativity.com/e-book.html

Gilbert, Danni. "Curious, Collaborative, Creativity: Applying Student-Centered Principles to Performing Ensembles". *Music Educators Journal* 103, no. 2 (2016): 27–34.

Hunter, Julie E. "The Rise of Women's Drumming in Africa: Performing Gender and Transforming Community in Southeastern Ghana". Ph.D., Brown University, 2012. https://repository.library.brown.edu/studio/item/bdr:297686/.

Johnson, David W. and Roger T. Johnson. "Making Cooperative Learning Work." *Theory Into Practice* 38, no. 2 (1999): 67–73.

Jonassen, David H. and Woei Hung. "Problem-Based Learning". In *Encyclopedia of the Sciences of Learning*, edited by Norbert M. Seel, 2687–90. New York: Springer, 2012.

"My Adirondack Home". YouTube Video, 3:34. Posted by M Hibit, February, 2017. Accessed January 1, 2018. www.youtube.com/watch?time_continue=2&v=kUocAvWgsHs.

Nettl, Bruno and Timothy Rommen. *Excursions in World Music*. 7th Edition. New York: Routledge, 2017.

Ruch, David. Personal communication with author on January 2, 2018.

Savery, John. "Overview of Problem-based Learning: Definitions and Distinctions." *International Journal of Problem-Based Learning* 1, no. 1 (2006): 9–20.

Shelemay, Kay Kaufman. *Soundscapes: Exploring Music in a Changing World*. 3rd Edition. New York: W.W. Norton & Company, 2015.

Smithsonian Folkways Recordings. Accessed January 19, 2018. https://folkways.si.edu

Songs to Keep: Treasures of an Adirondack Folk Collector. Directed by Paul Larson. Mountain Lake PBS, 2013. DVD.

Songs to Keep: The Adirondack North Country Songs Reimagined. Canton, NY: Traditional Arts of Upstate New York (TAUNY), 2013. Compact Disc.

Songs to Keep: Traditional Adirondack North Country Songs. Canton, NY: Traditional Arts of Upstate New York (TAUNY), 2013.

Titon, Jeff Todd. "Knowing Fieldwork." In *Shadows in the Field: New Perspectives for Fieldwork in Ethnomusicology*, edited by Gregory Barz and Timothy Cooley, 25–41. 2nd Edition. New York: Oxford University Press, 2008.

Titon, Jeff Todd, ed. *Worlds of Music: Music of the World's Peoples.* 6th Edition. Belmont, CA: Cengage Schirmer Learning, 2017.

TAUNY: Traditional Arts of Upstate New York. Accessed January 19, 2018. http://tauny.org.

"What is Project Based Learning?". Accessed January 1, 2018. www.bie.org/about/what_pbl.

Yang, Hon-Lun. "Teaching Music History at Hong Kong Baptist University: Problem-Based Learning and Outcome Based Teaching and Learning." *Journal of Music History Pedagogy* 4, no. 2 (2014): 329–32.

Younge, Paschal Yao. *Musical Traditions of Ghana, Volume 1: A Hand Book for Music Teachers and Instructors of West African Drumming.* Legon: University of Ghana School of Performing Arts, 1992.

Younge, Paschal Yao. *Music and Dance Traditions of Ghana: History, Performance and Teaching.* Jefferson, NC: McFarland & Company, 2011.

Part III
Music and Movement

9

Kinesics and Music Performance in the Introductory Music Class

SCOTT HORSINGTON

The first chapter in our Music and Movement section provides a look into an underexplored area. Movement is not typically discussed in music courses, but in this first chapter, Scott Horsington applies a Problem-based Learning (PBL) to a typical Introduction to Music course populated almost entirely by nonmusic, general education students. The PBL in this chapter, an exploration of kinesics, is an example of how a PBL can be used to explore a topic of great significance in music that is not directly related to the course curriculum. This additional dimension gave students a far deeper and more exciting look at what musicians do beyond practicing scales and learning chord progressions.

~

Introduction

We have all witnessed musicians moving while playing: the pianist who looks to the heavens, the "sniffing" cellist, and the infamous "flapping saxophone elbow." A tenor raises his hand while singing a high note, and a guitarist emphasizes her power chord with a jump. How are we to interpret these movements? Are these movements "convincing," driven by the music or the musician's internal experience of it, or are they simply for show, attempting to communicate divine inspiration or sublime musicianship? Regardless of which side of the debate one believes, these movements all represent kinesics – or, colloquially, "body language." A theory developed by Ray Birdwhistell, kinesics proposes that human communication uses all the senses, is coded in gestures, and that these codes are different across cultures (Birdwhistell 2007). These codes can be inferred and understood through careful observation. While we may dismiss these small actions as peripheral to the performance, they are nontheless considered part of the noncommunicative actions of kinesics.

At its most basic level, playing a musical instrument is a physical activity that recruits the nervous system and neural circuitry of physical movement to accomplish a non-movement goal, e.g. creating music. Learning to play an instrument requires mastery of the fine motor skills necessary to gain command of an instrument, namely through the smaller muscles of the arm, hands, and fingers. The work of actually embodying musical elements – things like tempo, style, dynamics, etc. – requires the use of the entire body and can be accomplished or observed in individuals who lack instrument-specific training. While much of learning music focuses on instrumental mastery, very little attention is paid to the physical embodiment of musical elements. Émile Jaques-Dalcroze, a Swiss music educator, recognized the value of this type of instruction, which led to the development of eurhythmics – a music education tool that uses gross movement to embody rhythm and meter.

Knowing this, it becomes clear that there is a certain degree of necessary movement in music performance. Chamber musicians breathe together, make eye contact, and move their bodies to ensure they are in sync. In the most obvious example, conductors attempt to communicate all aspects and qualities of music to their ensemble. Ironically, the conductor is completely removed from the actual production of musical sound, yet must use their entire body to convey or elicit the sound produced. Even dancers embody musical qualities in how they move to music – the same movement combination can undergo an observable, qualitative change simply by changing the style of musical accompaniment.

Through movement, musicians can convey meaning in something that is inherently nonverbal (assuming it is not a song with lyrics), from the basic musical elements of dynamics, tempo, or articulation, to higher-order elements such as style or emotional content. The Problem-Based Learning (PBL) in this chapter asks students to examine how this demonstrative behavior creates meaning for nonmusicians? How can they grasp intention through observation? On a more basic level, how can movement be used constructively and/or authentically to enhance music performance, specifically as it relates to communication when playing together? Exploring these questions adds a visual element to music that is not immediately obvious to the casual listener or audience member.

Background

I began teaching academic music courses at The College at Brockport, State University of New York (SUNY), in the fall of 2013. I'd already spent a year running a clarinet ensemble for the Music Studies program, and by the fall of 2013, I'd been hired to teach Music Theory and Introduction to Music. Introduction to Music, also known as "Intro" within the department, is a basic music literacy course that fulfills Brockport's Fine Art with Performance General

Education credit. No musical background is required. The course covers music fundamentals like reading in both clefs, scales and keys, basic rhythm reading, and basic chords, as well as requiring students to learn simple melodies on an instrument (typically keyboard, recorder, and/or ukulele). It is required for students pursuing a Music Minor or an Arts for Children Major, though the majority of students enroll to fulfill their General Education credits. As a result, Intro is the primary means by which Brockport's Music Studies program reaches the student body. All Intro classes are capped at 20 students, with multiple sections offered each semester. Both semesters in which I implemented my project had an enrollment of 19 students.

My particular curriculum introduces students to both the keyboard and the recorder – the keyboard for ease of understanding musical structures like scales and chords, and the recorder for its portability, simplicity, and the relationship of breath to duration when learning how to count rhythm, as well as differentiating articulation. At the time of the project, the course was a bit more theory-driven, but I've since scaled this back in favor of a more thorough grasp of basic music concepts and performing. In general, my primary goal is to make the course as relevant as possible to nonmusic students, and since most students will not continue in music-related coursework, I focus on what they can gain from the course that might be useful in their own lives. Typically, the course terminates in the construction of basic chords, interpreting pop chord symbols/guitar tabs, and self-accompaniment.

In conjunction with teaching academic coursework, I served as a staff musician for Brockport's Dance Department for six semesters, accompanying both Modern Dance and Ballet classes. Typically, dance classes involve the instructor demonstrating a particular combination of movements, usually referred to as a "phrase," while providing generic counts for tempo and accent. The musician then uses these counts as well as visual feedback from the movement sequence itself to identify the metric subdivision – simple or compound – as well as appropriate musical style. The counts alone are not enough, however, and some inherent quality of the movements themselves conveys subdivision and style. The style of musical accompaniment can actually influence the style of movement. For example, a movement phrase that is intended and instructed to be legato/sustained is subconsciously altered by the movers if the music suggests a more staccato or direct/sudden movement.

Although it may not be immediately obvious, all musicians inhabit a world of musical gestures. Such gestures are not explicitly taught in musical training but are subconsciously embodied by the student imitating their teacher, peers, or professionals they observe. Unable to speak in performance (most obviously for wind and brass players, due to having an instrument in their mouths), musicians, especially chamber musicians, must find alternative methods of communication. As mentioned in the introduction, conductors are the purest example of musical gesture, as they produce 0% of the musical sound during a performance, yet must communicate the most salient aspects of the music to an entire ensemble. Surface-level nonverbal communication includes eye contact and breath – eye contact ensures that relevant/similar/coincident parts are aware of each other and in the same place in the music (in case of becoming "lost"), and breath to convey entrances and tempo. In the case of breathing, the in-breath typically acts as a full beat pickup, and the subsequent rise and fall of the shoulders/rib cage/torso among all players serves as a bodily manifestation of the cue, similar to the pickup gesture and primary ictus in conducting. Beyond these more obvious forms of communication, there are more subtle gestures that indicate style and dynamics. These are often subconscious manifestations of an internalized understanding of the particular style of a piece, similar to how dancers subconsciously respond to the style of music used to accompany their movements.

These movements manifest themselves in solo performance as well. For example, everyone has seen a musician who moves too much, or one who moves too little, and how both extremes can detract from the music. While there is no clear answer as to what is the "correct" kind of movement in solo performance, the fact that it can (and does) manifest automatically to some degree suggests that it represents internalized musical understanding – the performer is "feeling" the music. Movement can also be inherent in some instrumental technique. Harpist and pedagogue Carlos Salzedo developed the idea that harpists' movements toward and away from the instrument should reflect rhythmic durations and musical style as well; the harp is the only instrument where sound is produced by moving away from the instrument body, necessitating that the player embodies the music since so much time is spent coming off and away from the strings (Owens 1993).

All of the above yield numerous questions: how does movement through physical space relate to rhythm, meter, and style? Having coached numerous youth chamber groups and conducted numerous ensembles at Brockport, these ideas were naturally part of my musical life and of particular interest to me. I wondered how students might explore the relationship between these elements in the music classroom. At the same time, observing dancers who didn't always "get it" when it came to moving in a way that reflects style and meter (particularly when jumping) indicated to me that this was an important pedagogical concept for anyone studying music. How can movement be used not only to teach musical concepts of rhythm, as is accomplished via eurhythmics, but to teach and enhance performance skills? In trying to identify a problem that beginner music students could solve in a classroom, it occurred to me that framing musical movement as a method of communication might be an ideal fit.

By providing students with opportunities to explore the relationship and uses of movement within music, and situations in which to observe how trained musicians communicate, they are able to look beyond the obvious aural components of music and see how it is embodied or communicated, and how it enhances or detracts from performance, hopefully providing them with tools for use in their own life. The problem was framed thus: How do musicians communicate? Since musicians typically can't communicate using speech while performing, what other means do they use to accomplish this critical task?

Project

Description

How do musicians communicate? In order to explore this question, I utilized a combination of in-class performance activities and observations of formal concerts with written reflections. For both semesters of implementation, departmental Student Learning Objectives (SLOs) and dimensions assigned to the course were as follows:

SLO #1 Demonstrate knowledge of music from a theoretical perspective:

1. Demonstrate knowledge of essential music theory terminology
2. Apply theoretical skills to analyze written or aural music
3. Identify connections between music and its theoretical components.

SLO #2 Ability to perform music:

1. Exhibit punctuality and reliable attendance at class/rehearsals and performances
2. Exhibit personal conduct and professional demeanor reflective of a performer (e.g. attention and focus on music during practice, rehearsal, and performance)
3. Executes assigned tasks including learning music and maintaining music copies or folders in a timely, responsible, and reliable fashion.

While the theory component typically covered essential skills like note and rhythm reading, construction of scales and keys, and understanding chords, the performance aspect of the course did little beyond basic music literacy. The goal of the project was to draw students' attention to, and to identify, the ways in which musicians communicate nonverbally. Nested within was the loftier goal of helping students developing basic cueing skills to improve their group performance.

Due to this higher proportion of nonmusic minor students enrolled in the courses, I elected to restructure the course so that upon completion, students would have an understanding of music that they could utilize in these social contexts. These skills include the basic understanding of chords and pop chord symbols and basic keyboard skills so that students could accompany themselves. Those interested in a more in-depth exploration of music theory already have the option to enroll in a dedicated upper-level theory course.

Problem versus Project?

In my opinion, this project blends elements of both Project- and Problem-based Learning. Since there is no concrete answer sought or product created, it does not fit the criteria for a project. It was framed more as "what have you learned or gained from your experience," "what did you discover," and "what is your opinion based on these items/what worked for you?" As novice musicians, the students can only answer these questions through their own experiences and experimentation. At the same time, it did contain some aspects of a project: the question posed is inherently a musical one that has been "solved" by those with musical training, e.g. there are correct and incorrect answers. For example, breathing and nodding are accepted and explicitly taught ways of communicating, while loudly stamping one's feet is not. Observing live performances to answer specific questions or prompts can be considered research, wherein students are identifying the "tried and true" methods used by professionals rather than developing their own personal solutions.

Perhaps the most appropriate label for this particular curriculum is "experiential learning" or learning by doing. According to Wurdinger and Carlson, experiential learning allows students to apply knowledge in situations where the instructor directs or facilitates learning (Wurdinger and Carlson 2009). In this case, the students solve the problem of musical communication in facilitated class activities, confirm their experience by observing experienced musicians, and then add this information to their personal musical "toolkit." While a typical PBL may seek to solve an external problem using knowledge within a particular field or context, this project uses the tools of music and tools of experience and observation that students already possess to improve their own abilities.

Process of Implementation

As previously stated, the course's in-class/lab activities were designed for novice musicians, and no formal knowledge of musical terminology or notation-reading skills were required. This allowed the first activity to occur

Table 9.1 PBL Work Distribution

In-Class	Outside of Class
Small group performances using classroom instruments	Concert attendance and written assignments

very early in the semester (typically the second or third meeting, often as a precursor to lessons on rhythm and meter). The first activity used simple classroom instruments like boomwhackers and small hand drums, which require no prior technical instruction. Students were then organized into groups of 3–4 and given the task of developing a brief rhythm composition. Prior to dividing the class into groups, students were led in a "boomwhacker orchestra," using call-and-response rhythms and obvious gestures by me to nonverbally direct the class in playing together. Upon dividing the class into groups, the only guidelines provided were that the students needed to come up with a piece in which they all played, with a clear beginning and a clear ending. They were given ten minutes to compose their piece, at which point they would perform it for the rest of the class. Prior to performing the piece, nonperforming students were asked to observe how the performing group chose to begin and end the piece within the guidelines. Following the initial round performances, students were then given another two minutes to modify their pieces with the stipulation that they could not begin or end the piece with any kind of verbal instructions. In addition, the ending of the piece had to be clear enough that the following group would be able to begin their piece immediately at the previous group's conclusion, "handing off" the performance like a relay race. Naturally, most groups settled on some sort of physical cuing. At this early stage, other common techniques included adding in rhythmic "layers" one at a time (eliminating the need to begin all together), having one player perform a brief introductory figure before other members joined in, or choosing a specific number of counts (e.g. play for 32 counts, though this requires all members to focus individually and count correctly).

In the original iteration of the project, this in-class group activity occurred on a second occasion with multiple repetitions of each group's composition, each requiring the students to add and communicate a musical element without verbal instructions. The initial stage replicated the original activity, i.e. a simple rhythm piece with nonverbal beginning and ending. The subsequent iterations included (1) unison beginning and ending, (2) a dynamic change, (3) a tempo change, (4) a change of rhythmic pattern, and (5+) various combinations of these elements. In general, groups relied on a leader who would signal changes using either a physical gesture or an aural cue.

The second main component required students to attend four concerts, writing a 500-word reflection after each. All students enrolled in Music Studies courses at Brockport are required to attend live concerts, and the written/observation portion of the project was easy to accomplish via this preexisting requirement. Performances were on-campus and included both student and professional ensembles. Students were prompted to observe nonverbal communication in performance, provide comparisons between different performing ensembles, and connect it to their experiences in the classroom.

The final component was a written assignment (without observation), which served as a capstone summary of the previous three. In it, students were asked to choose which form of communication they think is best and why – essentially enabling them to answer the question "how do musicians communicate?" directly from their own experience and observations, rather than through formal research or by providing a specific "correct" answer. Each assignment prompt focused on specific types or purposes of nonverbal communication demonstrated by the performers, drawing students' attention to different musical elements and giving them the opportunity to come to their own conclusions. The prompts were as follows:

Paper 1:

What were your expectations for this concert, and why? Were they met, exceeded, or not met? Observe the performers. What are some ways that they communicate with each other nonverbally? Does it contribute to the performance, or take away from the performance? Why do you think so?

Paper 2:

In your previous paper, you watched for nonverbal communication between the performers. Watch for it again in this performance, and compare it to the other performance you saw. Did these performers use similar methods to communicate with each other? Did they do anything different than the other performers from your last concert? Are there differences or changes in tempo (speed) or dynamics (volume) in the music, and if so, how do they show it to each other?

Now, think about your group composition activities from class. In these groups, you are required to play with classmates without using speech. What techniques did you or other group members use to communicate with each other while playing? Be explicit and descriptive! At this concert, did you notice any of the same methods being used by the performers?

Paper 3:

For this paper, you will again look for nonverbal communication during the performance. In your last paper, you observed performers communicating changes in dynamics and tempo, as well as any similarities between the types of communication these musicians used and what you used during class activities. This time, take a look at how the movements of the musicians reflect what is happening in the music. In other words, how do they show the music's style? When it's fast, how do they move differently than when it's slow? What about loud versus soft? What about smooth and gentle versus fast and staccato? These are just a few examples, but your main objective is to notice if there is any relationship to *how* musicians move/communicate and the *style* of the music.

In your opinion, which group or performers did the best job at showing the style of the music, and why? Also, remember to give a personal reaction or critique of the performance. What did you like or dislike, and why? Did you like certain groups or songs more than others? Why?

Paper 4:

The fourth paper is a synthesis of your first three papers. Now that you've seen a number of concerts, what ways have you seen musicians communicate nonverbally? Of what you have seen, which way do you think is the best/most effective? In class, you've spent time playing with your classmates and experimenting with the different types of nonverbal communication you've observed. Of what you've tried, which was the easiest?

Keep in mind there are TWO questions here: first, from your observations, what form of nonverbal communication looks the most effective? Second, from your own experiences in class, what way was the easiest for you personally? Last, but not least, if you could think of one word or phrase to describe the ways musicians communicate (music aside), what word or phrase would you choose?

In the second implementation of the project, in-class activities occurred on three occasions rather than two, and included a discussion period after the fourth required concert but prior to its due date. This allowed students an opportunity to see what conclusions their peers came to, as well as identify common themes or ideas.

Case Study Examples

Below are some examples of student written work from the third and fourth written assignments. In both semesters of implementation, this particular concert featured a large ensemble with conductor, whereas earlier concerts featured smaller chamber groups. As a result, all examples below refer to conducting as a form of nonverbal communication.

After taking this class and watching several concerts, I have come to the conclusion that nonverbal communication is incredibly difficult and there is no one set way that is better than the others, it is just based on personal preference. However, I do believe that having a conductor to keep everyone on beat and remind them when and where changes need to be made is a far more effective method than letting the players figure it out for themselves. It is doable without a conductor; however, it would most likely take far more practice and would require good chemistry between the players so they know each other's style, on top of all this there is still far more room for error when there is no leader.

Cameron

Another movement that I noticed from the conductors was that when songs needed to get louder the conductors would widen their arm movements when they conducted the piece. When songs needed to get softer, the conductors move their arms closer to their sides while waving their batons.

Lauren

The movements of the conductors greatly reflect what is actually happening in the piece. When it comes to the gesture of the conductor, the most important thing the conductor can control is volume. Large sweeping motions are typically used for loud sections, while small movements are used to control the more quiet sections... When staccato was present in a piece, the conductor would gesture short and fast movements. This differs from legato, which refers to long and connected notes. When this is in the piece, the conductor is usually more fluid in their presentation...

I believe that the most significant use of nonverbal communication is the use of hand motions because it is most effective in making sure that everyone is on the same page at all times... Overall, I found this concert to be very engaging and I had a fun time attending it.

Dan

In my intro to music class, we practiced similar methods of nonverbal communication.... For the group that I was in, we had one person act like a conductor to control our tempo, loudness and when we start and stop. We would all have to look or listen to him in order to know what we were supposed to do. It wasn't very complicated. We simply mimicked him and that was it. It wasn't nearly as complicated as what the conductor was doing on stage but it gave us a basic idea of what it was like. Although this concert wasn't my favorite, I enjoyed studying the conductor to see how he communicates and of course, I really enjoyed the opera singer.

Nick

...[W]hen the only form of communication between when to start and stop was a look at each other, or a count off, there was room for error and miscommunication. On the other hand, when there was one person whose entire job was leading a group to try and make sure that everyone was together and that everyone was getting the same messages as to what and when to play at the same time there was less room for error.... [F]rom what I observed, the most effective version of nonverbal communication that musicians use is to have someone standing in front of them...

The conductor uses many different ways to show the ensemble what they should be doing in order to convey whatever message it is that the composer intended to express. If the conductor is looking to control the dynamic of a piece, as you did many times in this performance, they would do it by controlling the broadness of their stroke when keeping the beat, for example if they wanted to increase the volume they would broaden their stoke showing those performing that they should not be holding back as much like they would if the conductor were to be using smaller almost hushed strokes to keep the beat, expressing that the volume should be confined to an almost smaller area.

Walden

Outcomes/Assessment

Student Assessment

Students were not required to complete a formal assessment of the project. As described above, the final component of the project – the fourth reflection – tasked the students with drawing their own conclusions as to what method of nonverbal communication worked the best, both for the in-class groups and in their personal observations of live performances. While trained musicians can easily identify the best methods of communication, I did not want to suggest a definitive answer or solution, as this could render some conclusions incorrect. This was antithetical to the point of the project, which was to simply draw the attention of novice musicians to the subtle body language used by experienced musicians and to help develop or experience that skill in their own performances. The fact that the majority of students were able to "solve" the problem, draw a conclusion, and give a definitive answer showed that the project worked, at least in the capacity of students' abilities to observe, recognize, and describe nonverbal communication among musicians.

In addition to fulfilling the writing requirement for the course, the concert attendance writing prompts provided students with something to look for or pay attention to while attending concerts, as the typical student may not find the music engaging or something they would attend by choice (i.e. it promotes more active listening). This being the case, in the future, I am interested in receiving student input on the in-class activity portion only. The observations made in concerts are contingent on student experiences in class, and since the activities are the true "meat" of the project, I am interested primarily in their experiences therein.

My Assessment

In general, the project was a success. In my assessment of the project, I found that students generally grasped the concept, identified similar things, and came to similar conclusions about nonverbal communication in music performance. As one would expect in an introductory-level course, some students were hesitant to fully participate in classroom activities, but I believe this to be rooted more in the personality of the students, their level of investment in the course, and/or their musical experience prior to enrolling in the course, rather than a product of difficulty. Despite hesitation, the majority of students "got it," especially by the fourth or fifth time participating in the classroom activities as well as from watching live performances, and there were no major moments of failure. However, I believe the project did not go far enough, and a more complete or in-depth exploration of nonverbal communication could certainly be undertaken in future iterations. This was partly due to a more theory-heavy content focus that I have since abandoned in favor of more performance experiences.

In the future, I'd like to expand the project and make it part of the standard course curriculum, as it addresses skills that could be used in a nonmusical/casual music context. Movement is inherently tied to music, but it is hardly ever addressed or discussed in the music classroom, whether it be an introductory-level course such as the one described herein, private instrument instruction, or even in the standard performing ensemble (with the exception of chamber music). This is particularly true in the context of Introduction to Music: so much time is spent on reading notation, gaining basic literacy, and exploring more advanced theoretical structures that are better saved for a Music Theory course that the value of exploring movement as it relates to performance is overlooked.

As stated above, future iterations of the project will require more class time devoted to playing together, both in general activities such as using boom-whackers and simple percussion, and in performing on the graded instruments (recorder and piano). It may also be beneficial to repeat the activity more often, especially when written assignment due dates are approaching. This would give students both an opportunity to "test out" what they've observed and can prime them for upcoming observations. This may also be useful for inciting more regular discussion around how to play together.

Since many students arrived at the conclusion that using a conductor was the best form of nonverbal communication, the writing prompts could be modified to focus more heavily on the in-class experience of playing together. While conducting does seem to be the most obvious solution to the problem of communication, this could theoretically be interpreted by students as the "correct" answer, thus missing the point of exploring communication between performing musicians and how the students might use the same tools or skills. This could also be mitigated by providing opportunities to observe performances outside the context of the traditional concert hall or academic music concert (for example, videos of other musical styles or cultural/world music traditions). Another alternative could be assigning the final reflection as part of a graded in-class performance so that students take more ownership of the types of communication they observed and can reflect on it subjectively, rather than relating their experiences to "what professionals do."

The in-class performance activities may have been lacking in enough variety or simply too repetitive. Aside from the changing limitations/requirements imposed during class performances, these activities were always identical: the students composed rhythm pieces in groups using boomwhackers and hand drums. There could certainly be more variation in how these performance experiences are structured (group size, instrumentation, form, length, etc.).

The written reflections could also be expanded to include topics like stage presence, pre- and post-performance body language (entering and exiting the stage, behavior of the performers prior to playing, bowing after performing), and even response/reaction of the performers to mistakes (should any occur). While not explicitly related to nonverbal communication between performing musicians, these "soft" aspects of music performance are observable, impact the performance and the audience's perception of it, and can be imitated by students in their own performance.

Use of appropriate cuing, nonverbal communication, and "saving face" when mistakes are made could even become a metric for graded performances. I am also interested in using the project as a launchpad for exploring nonverbal communication in everyday life, as this may enhance students' understanding of it. This could include watching performers of popular music in addition to attending live concerts, or even pushing the boundary as far as people-watching normal conversations (identifying posture, gesture, how meaning is conveyed, etc. and tying it back to how these same behaviors can be applied in music). Furthermore, all of these observations and experiences could be related to larger social contexts, like how music enhances or detracts from certain scenes, environments, or atmospheres, whether they be in the entertainment industry or public spaces.

1. These concepts have been explored by earlier music pedagogues, the most obvious of whom is Dalcroze.

Bibliography

Birdwhistell, Ray L. *Kinesics and Context: Essays on Body Motion Communication*. Philadelphia: University of Pennsylvania Press, 2007 [1970].

"Dalcroze Society of America - Welcome to the 2018 DSA National Conference!" *Dalcroze Society of America - Welcome to the 2018 DSA National Conference!*, dalcrozeusa.org/

Owens, Dewey. *Carlos Salzedo, from Aeolian to Thunder: a Biography*. Chiago, IL: Lyon & Healy Harps, 1993.

Wurdinger, Scott D. and Julie Carlson. *Teaching for Experiential Learning: Five Approaches That Work*. New York: Rowman and Littlefield, 2009.

10
Using Movement as a Vehicle for Problem-Based Learning in Introductory Music Courses

TAMARA WILCOX

In the second of our Music and Movement Problem-based Learnings, Tamara explores an interdisciplinary and integrative approach to the task, having students find their musical voice through movement. Rather than producing a written product, students were asked to create movements to music as their culminating midterm and final assignments called "plastique." Tamara demonstrates integration of the two areas by using a spiral curriculum technique of bringing each level a bit deeper and further until they were well out of the student's comfort zone. Tamara then shares her thoughts about the process and success of her case studies as well as an assessment at the end.

> The best method of teaching is that which, from the start, offers the pupil a problem which neither his memory nor his instinct for imitation can help him to solve.
>
> —E. Jaques-Dalcroze, *Rhythm Music & Education* (1921, p. 27)

~

Why Movement?

After spending years as a professional dance musician, I view music and movement as an inseparable pair. Because they share so many of the same fundamental elements such as rhythm, phrasing, energy/dynamics, form, range, and time/space, I have found, both as a performer and as an educator, that each informs the other. Consequently, I find myself unable to teach either discipline without the inclusion of its intrinsic counterpart.

Movement is not a new component of music education. It was most notably the 20th-century Swiss music educator Émile Jaques-Dalcroze who developed a new music pedagogy based on his discoveries and research into the relationship between music and movement.

To sum up: music is composed of sound and movement. Sound is a form of movement of a secondary, rhythm of a primary, order. Musical studies should therefore be preceded by exercises in movement. Every limb – first separately, then simultaneously, finally the whole body – should be set in rhythmic motion; the resulting formations, i.e. the relations between the energy, space, and time involved, being carefully collated and regulated.

(Jaques-Dalcroze 1921, 44)

There have also been others whose research and observation led to similar conclusions.

Alexandra Pierce, Emerita Research Professor of Music and Movement at the University of Redlands (Pierce 2007, 4), credits the late Dr. Ida Rolf with having been a primary influence on her own work in the field of music and movement for musicians. Dr. Rolf is known for developing the system of "Structural Integration," which is defined as "a system of manual therapy and sensorimotor education that purports to improve human biomechanical functioning as a whole" (Jacobson, 2011, 775). Pierce, describing the genesis of her own research, states,

I had sensed, but did not yet understand, that moving the beat, melody, or phrase propelled players, even reluctant ones, into a music-infused, ear-awakened awareness. The beat, for instance, was no longer just a bossy metronome tick. When the musical quality of the beat became vivid as movement and reverberated through a responsive body rather than, say, just an arm, a corresponding shift in musical expression could be expected.

(2007, 2)

Finally, it should be noted that recent studies in 21st-century neuroscience research are confirming what Dalcroze, Pierce, and like-minded others have intuitively known about this relationship all along. One recent McGill University neuroscience study indicates that (1) the motor system in the brain plays a key role in our ability to perceive sound, and (2) when rhythmic movement is involved, our sound perceptions are sharper and more discriminatory (Morillon and Baillet 2017, E8913).

Background Information

The course in which I have experimented with a music/movement Problem-Based Learning (PBL) approach is Introduction to Music, an introductory general education fine arts course with performance emphasis at The College at Brockport, SUNY. This course is open to any student with no prerequisite and serves as the gateway course to a minor in Music Studies. The course is taught with the assumption that the students enrolled have absolutely no prior music education or experience (even though some of them actually do). It is up to each course instructor to choose which instrument(s) they would like to include to fulfill the performance requirement. In my sections, I utilize piano as the primary instrument of performance, although I also include a vocal component. I chose to implement a PBL approach in this course because it easily lends itself to a laboratory setting for exploration using movement and music. I also enjoy the challenge of finding new and more effective ways to facilitate the evolution of novices toward music literacy, and awaken in them the ability to use music as a medium of self-expression.

The Music Studies Student Learning Outcomes for this course are as follows:

Demonstrate Knowledge of Music from a Theoretical Perspective
Demonstrate Knowledge of Essential Music Theory Terminology

- Apply theoretical skills to analyze written or aural music
- Identify connections between music and its theoretical components

The Student Learning Objectives for This Course Include

- Counting and performing rhythms in simple and compound meters consisting of note values of eighth notes/rests through whole notes/rest
- Read notes in treble and bass clef and perform on keyboard and/or recorder and/or sing on tonal syllables
- Playing simple melodies on an instrument
- Constructing intervals and triads and playing them on an instrument
- Transposing music from key to another and playing on an instrument
- Writing diatonic triads on a staff and play on keyboard from popular notation and Roman numerals
- Writing basic triads on a staff in five major keys
- Writing the Circle of Fifths to include five major and minor keys
- Writing a short paper reflecting the writing conventions of the disciplinary area
- Demonstrate understanding of at least one principal form of artistic expression and the creative process inherent therein
- Demonstrate competence in the analytical tools used to interpret that form
- Actively participate in artistic activities specifically related to one or more artistic form

In addition, Introduction to Music has a writing requirement in order to maintain its status as a General Education course. This requirement is fulfilled through the completion of three concert reflections in which students must attend three live departmental concerts and then articulate their observations in narrative form using their expanding repertoire of musical terms.

During this semester-long course, two-thirds of the weekly class time was spent in the keyboard lab and one-third was spent in a self-designated "movement lab" (another classroom with ample movement space and a piano). Students spent time in the keyboard lab learning: rhythm, solfege, and keyboard improvisation warm ups; guided keyboard practice; work with scales and chords; playing simple melodies with chordal accompaniment; playing easy selections from the standard repertoire; introduction to the fundamentals of music and basic music theory; and learning about piano technique and practice strategies. Time spent in the movement lab was devoted to the implementation of the PBL approach and will be discussed in the remainder of this chapter.

Taking a PBL Approach

I have been integrating movement into my music pedagogy practices since I began teaching. In my introductory music courses, for example, I frequently use movement to help students establish their internal pulse, find a sense of duple versus triple beat divisions, understand common and uncommon metric groupings and metric accents, feel the continuity of a musical phrase from beginning to end, more clearly express dynamic nuance, and experiment with various types of articulation. If I am teaching a piano lesson and my student is stumbling over a rhythm, struggling to decide how to shape a phrase, or feeling uninspired, I will address these issues through a spontaneous movement experience. Nine out of ten times, the problem solves itself once the student lets their body lead.

The invitation to write this chapter led me to reevaluate and rethink exactly how I was orchestrating the integration of movement. I started by asking myself a series of questions and revisiting some of my initial course foundations. How can I more effectively create an atmosphere for a PBL application in my course? How can I provide more opportunities for PBL in my course? How can I allow more time for students to be engaged in learning using PBL in my course? Was it possible to implement PBL in an applied music setting with movement as the vehicle?

According to Yang, PBL "uses problems as an initiative to set out the learning process that result in a vibrant and active learning environment, leading to the development of higher order cognitive skills" (2014, 330). She highlights attributes of students working in a PBL atmosphere: heightened curiosity, a greater sense of curricular relevance, and an increased ability to comprehensively integrate the various elements of the course.

I also recalled the words of psychologist Jerome Bruner:

> It is my hunch that it is only through the exercise of problem solving and the effort of discovery that one learns the working heuristics of discovery; the more one has practice, the more likely one is to generalize what one has learned into a style of problem solving or inquiry that serves for any kind of task encountered – or almost any kind of task.
>
> (Bruner 1979, 94)

A performance-oriented course is one in which the body is being experienced as a vehicle for sharpening musical awareness, igniting cognition, and fostering self-expression, all through a process of discovery. Overall student success, therefore, could certainly be best supported through a succession of problems upon which to build. Providing students with ample opportunities to navigate simple problems before expecting them to address more complex problems is also essential to a successful PBL environment. This sentiment has been echoed by cellist Yo-Yo Ma, "When a problem is complex, you become tense. But when you break it down…you can approach each element without stress" (Olmstead, 2006, 14).

Since I was utilizing an interdisciplinary approach, I needed to clarify what problem-solving in a movement context would look like. According to McCutchen, "Problem solving in dance requires creative thinking and processing. Movement exploration is one of the first uses of problem solving" (2006, 175). McCutchen then discusses two additional uses of problem-solving in dance: experimenting and improvising. She emphasizes that experimenting and improvising "take an inquiring, evolutionary, loosely structured approach." As a point of contrast, what a PBL approach to movement would *not* be, for example, is a technique class where the instructor shows a combination and the students are expected to copy/imitate what they see. McCutchen goes on to draw comparisons between the creative process and the scientific process (177).

> Both processes gather information, identify potential problems, seek solutions, and conclude the investigation. Both processes usually go step by step, but not always are the steps linear; sometimes they spiral back through to pick up previous steps. By the end of each process…the investigator has used higher-order thinking along with inductive and deductive reasoning.
>
> (McCutchen, 177)

Allowing students enough time for movement exploration, experimentation, and improvisation is also essential for PBL. Savery (2006, 12) echoes McCutchen's ideas with his description of PBL as a "selection of ill-structured problems."

In clarifying PBL for myself, there were two key points of distinction that aided me significantly in defining this approach. First, Boud and Feletti, in their 1997 book, *The Challenge of Problem-Based Learning* (cited in Savery 11), reminded readers that PBL was not merely teaching problem-solving, but rather an approach to curriculum design. Second, Boud and Feletti state, PBL "is a way of conceiving of the curriculum as being centered upon key problems in professional practice" (quoted in 2014, 1).

Finally, I asked myself what PBL might look like in an applied music setting, where real-world problems include technique and music interpretation. Author Gerald Klickstein discusses such problems faced by performing artists in his book *The Musician's Way*.

> Artistic problems, however, cry out for a more adventurous sort of thinking, one that can engage difficulties from disparate angles and generate many promising solutions. That's where divergent thinking comes in. When you let your thoughts diverge, you perceive problems from compound viewpoints. You leave conventional categories behind and hunt for ideas by posing open-ended questions. 'What if I tried it this way?' you wonder, unlike convergent thinkers, who thirst for 'the right answers.' Actually, divergent thinking is more about asking questions than finding answers.
>
> (2009, 54–55)

Music Professor Daniel Stevens also discusses similar problems faced by performing artists in his article "Problem-Based Learning in the Music Classroom" in which he states,

> I first encountered PBL as a graduate piano student, when my teacher circled a single note in a Bach Sinfonia and asked me to return next week to explain and defend how long the note should be held. To answer this question, I drew on my knowledge of Baroque articulation, counterpoint, and dissonance treatment….By engaging in a real problem and drawing on multiple sources of knowledge to find a solution, I learned not only how to articulate the note in question but many others as well.
>
> (2014, 1)

Process

The problem I tasked my students with exploring was to find their own musical voice and to find it through the vehicle of movement. The challenge of sculpting one's unique artistic musical product from a two-dimensional score is a real-world problem any performing artist faces every time they learn and perform a piece of music. And, as discussed earlier in this chapter, movement has been successfully shown to be an organic means of ushering forth one's innate and most genuine sense of musicality. At the end of the semester, the students would present what they discovered as a small group in the form of a choreographic interpretation of their final piano repertoire piece. This presentation would require the students to draw upon both their in-class movement experiences in the movement lab and their classroom theoretical knowledge. This culminating presentation is what Jaques-Dalcroze called "*moving* or *living plastic*" (1921, 147).

> Once the limbs are trained, once the senses and mind have been awakened by rhythm, the nervous resistances eliminated, and the divers forces of the organism connected by a continuous and powerful current, it becomes necessary to complete the muscular sense, the feeling for space and familiarity with its laws – as well as that for shades of time – by the acquisition of aesthetic qualities and of the instinct for divining the results certain movements will produce on others, and which enable the plastic artist to realise with his limbs gestures and attitudes he has previously imagined.
>
> (148)

Students were given time in the movement lab each week to explore, experiment, and improvise (McCutchen 2006, 94). In addition, the class participated in weekly movement lab experiences intended to awaken and inspire their musicality through their innate body intelligence. Students in this context need a safe environment, encouragement, and the leeway to try and try again. The individual nature of personal embodiment presents as a wide parameter of interpretive differences and nuanced distinctions.

Examples of Movement Experiences What follows are some examples of the types of movement experiences the class did in the movement lab, which allows students, as discussed earlier, to navigate simpler problems before more comprehensive problems. These are presented in table form in order to distinguish between a more traditional versus a more PBL approach.

Midterm Presentation The midterm PBL "plastique" presentation was the keyboard piece they were playing for their midterm keyboard playing assessment. This piece was a simple melody with chordal accompaniment. In the embodiment of the left hand, the primary movement objective is rhythmic in nature. The challenge for the students in the keyboard lab with chordal pieces is transitioning between chords. Specific keyboard strategies are addressed while in the keyboard lab, and the movement lab experience will address the rhythm of

Table 10.1 Traditional vs. PBL Models of Teaching with Music through Movement

Traditional	PBL
Ask students to clap to the beat (while teacher accompanies on piano). If students are struggling, teacher sings the tune and demonstrates clapping to the beat.	Ask students to find a way to use their arms/hands to embody both the point of sound (where they hear the macro beat reoccurring) and the full expanse of the beat (time in between where the beats happen). To encourage discovery, repeat this activity a few times and ask students to find at least two different ways they could possibly embody this. (Clapping is only one possibility.) This is a first step in upper-body coordination and finding the connection between musical time and actual space. Also, while accompanying the students on piano, periodically stop playing and then come back in as if you had played through the silence so that students also learn to audiate the beat themselves, supporting their connection to their sense of inner pulse. * Why arms/hands first? Bringing the hands/arms together is part of the core/distal movement pattern (Studd and Cox 2013, 55), which is the first movement pattern in the sequence of human development, therefore easiest to coordinate.
Ask students to step to the beat (while teacher accompanies on piano). If students are struggling, teacher sings the tune and demonstrates walking to the beat.	Ask students to find a way to move through space in such a way that both the point of sound and the full expanse of the beat are embodied. To encourage discovery, repeat this activity a few times and ask students to find at least two different ways they could possibly embody this. (Walking is only one possibility.) * Why clap before step? Clapping is a core/distal movement pattern (Studd and Cox 2013, 55), and walking is a cross-lateral movement pattern (59). The former is more primal (happens earlier developmentally) and therefore easier for the human body to coordinate.

Traditional	PBL
Ask students to clap the beat and its duple division along with the music they hear (teacher accompanies on piano). * Do the same for triple divisions.	Ask students to, together in pairs, find a way to represent the full expanse of a beat and its duple division (teacher does not accompany). Ask each group to find at least three ways to embody this. They will have to get in touch with their own inner pulse and collaboratively explore tempo, space, and metric accent. * For triple divisions, ask students to work in trios.
Teacher plays a tune and then asks the class if it is in a simple duple meter or a simple triple meter (students may indicate by raising hands).	Students work in small groups. They listen to the music being played and are encouraged to move freely, either through the space or around a stationary spine. After ample opportunity to listen and explore, the students are given time to create a simple group embodiment of the meter. They have already explored upper-body movement, lower-body movement, and movement through space. They are encouraged to try new ways of embodying the music.
Teacher plays a simple song consisting of two phrases. She plays a crescendo from the beginning to the end of the first phrase and then a decrescendo from the beginning of the second phrase to the end. She asks the students which they heard first/second, the crescendo or the decrescendo.	Students work in the same small groups. They are encouraged to move freely as they listen while the teacher plays the simple song multiple times. They are asked to find ways to embody the change in dynamics/change in energy. Once they look as if they have found some ideas, the teacher experiments with other dynamic ideas for the same simple song (start with decrescendo and end with crescendo, for example) and other songs expressing different dynamic qualities.
Teacher plays a simple song and asks students to raise their hand when they hear the ending of one phrase and beginning of another.	Students work in small groups. As teacher plays simple song, students are encouraged to find multiple ways of using their bodies (both stationary and moving through the space) to articulate through their embodiment, the beginning, duration, ending, and new beginning of each phrase.

the chording as well as the coordination of the chordal rhythm with the melody line. In the embodiment of the right hand, the primary movement objective includes rhythm and phrasing. (In the keyboard lab, additional objectives include use of correct fingering in both melody and chords, pitch/key accuracy, left-hand shifting, and a new skill of alternate chord positions requiring a greater level of finger independence.)

We began with each hand separately. I play the piece on the piano while students work in groups to embody the left hand and the right hand in turn. They experiment with the use of upper appendages, lower appendages, body percussion, movement through space, and movement around a stationary spine. Once students feel confident with this, we work on embodying both the left and the right hands simultaneously.

Final Presentation

The final PBL "plastique" presentation was the keyboard piece they were playing for their final keyboard playing assessment. The final piano repertoire piano solo movement embodiment goals included rhythm (different rhythms in the left and the right hands), phrasing, dynamics, and range of motion. The keyboard lab piano performance goals included, additionally, independence of each hand, finger independence, pitch/key accuracy, keyboard range, shifting, both contrary and parallel motion, finger transfers (over and under), and use of correct fingering. As before, we began with each hand separately. I play the piece on the piano while students work in groups to embody the left hand and the right hand in turn. They experiment with the use of upper appendages, lower appendages, body percussion, movement through space, and movement around a stationary spine. Once students feel confident with this, we work on embodying both the left and the right hands simultaneously. The added challenge in this experience is that the left hand part is not just chords on the downbeats, but rather an independent accompaniment part with some counterpoint as well. In addition, the use of dynamics and a greater pitch range add even more opportunities for discovery and expression.

Case Studies

Case Study #1: Michael, Jimmy, and Zak

Michael and Jimmy were both the same type of learners. Neither excelled at written work or written exams, but both put their hearts into all other aspects of class and were rarely absent. Both quickly embraced the challenges they faced in the movement lab. Zak was the opposite. He excelled at written work and written exams but was clearly challenged in the movement lab. Of the three, Zak struggled the most to coordinate and organize his body in order to find the pathway to his unique musical voice. The beauty was that Michael and Jimmy were so exuberant and daring that it encouraged Zak, and he took risks that I feel he would not have otherwise. Zak's movement qualities were more thoughtful and reserved, while Michael's and Jimmy's were more gregarious and bold. This translated into each of their approaches to the keyboard as well. I find that each student has their own "default" approach to the keyboard. When I work with them, I try to take them beyond their own comfort zone. One marvelous aspect of this collaborative work is that Michael, Jimmy, and Zak did this for each other.

Case Study #2: Justin and Terry

Justin and Terry were both affable students and quickly caught on to class concepts. However, due to other life demands, both often missed class. When they were present for the movement lab, they were both focused on the tasks at hand. However, due to the fact that they missed so many opportunities for exploratory time on the PBL presentation and the additional class movement explorations (and they obviously did not meet together outside of class) meant that their final presentation was not as developed as were others in the class. From this evidence, I would emphasize the importance of allowing all students ample time throughout the course of the semester to both freely explore/work on their PBL presentation, and time to participate in a series of PBL movement experiences as they evolve.

Assessment

Ideas to Increase Effectiveness

In order for students to feel comfortable working through movement, it is essential, as mentioned above, that they have designated class time each week to explore in a movement lab setting. For many of them, it is a first time making mind-body connections and music-movement connections. Consequently, most will feel a bit awkward and maybe even silly at first. Furthermore, even students who have movement backgrounds (such as dance majors) need time to find their own authentic kinesthetic responses in order to express their musicality through movement.

As discussed above, the nature of the experiences in the movement lab must be PBL in nature. If the teacher dictates what the students are to do and how they are to do it, they will not have the opportunity to follow their own path to discovery and find and then be able to express their own unique musical voice.

Successes

It was most exciting to witness stages of embodiment from the movement lab carry over to the keyboard lab and support the students' success in keyboard performance and theoretical understanding. As mentioned above, most students have their own "default" approach to the keyboard. In piano lessons, I use a variety of strategies to help them experiment with playing outside their comfort zones. One of these strategies is movement. Some of my "heavy-handed" players such as Michael and Jimmy, who struggled with dynamic control, were able to produce a much wider dynamic palette by the end of semester. Likewise, some of my quiet players, such as Zak, who felt very uncomfortable going beyond what might be described as mezzo-piano, by the end of semester reached a full-fledged fortissimo.

The PBL presentation transferred to other projects in the classroom. At the end of the semester, students had a project in the keyboard lab. Working with a partner, their challenge was to listen to the partner perform their final piano repertoire piece and then problem-solve in order to help their partner improve. They had to suggest five specific practice/performance strategies that they could try to solve the problem. Later, in their final performance, students had to ask the same question of themselves. Some strategies arose from guided practice experiences we had done as a class (later in the semester, we generated a list as a class based upon these experiences). Some strategies arose from the students' creative thinking and problem-solving on their own. However, the PBL success from my perspective was that although I never included our movement lab work as a piano practice/performance strategy list, several of the students themselves did. Over half the class used this suggestion with one another and then later in their own final self-assessment. They felt that the PBL movement work helped them in their piano performance and theoretical understanding. That was the integration I was hoping for.

Bibliography

Bruner, Jerome. *On Knowing: Essays for the Left Hand*, 2nd Edition. Cambridge, MA: Harvard University Press, 1979.

Jacobson, Eric. "Structural Integration: Origins and Development." *The Journal of Alternative and Complementary Medicine* 17, no. 9 (2011): 775–80.

Jaques-Dalcroze, Emile. Rhythm Music & Education. Burgess Hill: Burnetts Printing Works, 1921.

Klickstein, Gerald. *The Musician's Way*. New York: Oxford University Press, 2009.

McCutchen, Brenda Pugh. *Teaching Dance as Art in Education*. Champaign, IL: Human Kinetics, 2006.

Morillon, Benjamin and Sylvain Baillet. "Motor Origin of Temporal Predictions in Auditory Attention." *PNAS* 114, no. 42 (October 2017): E8913–E8921.

Olmstead, Mary. *Yo-Yo Ma*. Chicago, IL: Raintree, 2006.

Pierce, Alexandra. *Deepening Musical Performance through Movement*. Bloomington: Indiana University Press, 2007.

Savery, John. "Overview of Problem-based Learning: Definitions and Distinctions." *Interdisciplinary Journal of Problem-Based Learning* 1, no. 1 (Spring 2006): 9–20.

Stevens, Daniel. "Problem-Based Learning in the Music Classroom, a Rationale." *Engaging Students: An Unconference and Journal on Classroom Music Pedagogy* 2, (2014): 1–6.

Studd, Karen and Laura Cox. *Every Body Is A Body*. Indianapolis, IN: Dog Ear Publishing, 2013.

Yang, Hon-Lun. "Teaching Music History at Hong Kong Baptist University: Problem-Based learning and Outcome-Based Teaching and Learning." *Journal of Music History Pedagogy*, 4 no. 2 (2014): 329–32.

Part IV
Music Theory and Education

11
Problem-Based "Projects" in the Music Education Class

NATALIE SARRAZIN

This chapter is the first in our final section of the volume involving Music Theory and Education. In this case study, Natalie implements an interdisciplinary Problem-Based Learning using the parameters of Music, Civic Responsibility, and Music Education, in which students integrate all three areas to produce lesson plans which are taught in actual classrooms. The issue of problem- versus project-based is explored, as well as the fact that this case study was included in two different semesters with varying outcomes in each. In the end, Natalie assesses the successes and challenges in each implementation, and describes which process yielded the best results.

Introduction

Like many of my other colleagues contributing to this book, my initial reaction to Problem-based Learning (PBL) spurred a number of emotions, ranging from trepidation to excitement. I struggled with the idea of how I might implement such a dramatic change in my course curriculum and put in a great deal of thought concerning the PBL process, the outcomes I desired, and generally how I might be able to fit such a project into an already-packed schedule. Several critical questions came to mind: How might I craft a substantial enough assignment that would not only enhance learning in the classroom but also do justice to the concept of PBL itself? Would I be able to change my teaching style in order to accommodate this new learning process? How might students react to such a change given their general dislike for group work?

Once I settled on reasonable answers to these questions, my next challenge was to select a course in which to implement the PBL. Although an ethnomusicologist by PhD, I am a music educator as well and teach courses in both fields. I had to make a decision as to which course would work best for piloting this technique. Initially, I suspected that a PBL would be much easier to implement in an ethnomusicology or other humanities course, something which the case studies in this book tend to corroborate. However, I was also teaching a Music Education course, so I decided to attempt the PBL in the more challenging and more practically based course first.

The course I used was entitled Music and the Child, an upper-division general music pedagogy course specifically designed for students in the Arts for Children (AFC) major. The AFC major is an interdisciplinary major in which students are required to take two courses in each of the four main arts areas (theater, dance, music, and visual art), while specializing in one of those arts and taking an additional 21 credits in that specialty area. In other words, they are not music, visual art, or dance majors per se but gain experience in at least two courses in each arts area and accumulate a large number of classes in their specialty area. One additional factor concerning the student class profile is that the majority of these students are enrolled in the College's Education Certification program and will graduate with the credentials necessary to teach K–6 in New York State.

Curricular Strategy for the PBL

Music and the Child, as previously mentioned, is the second music course required of all AFC majors, although several non-AFC students occasionally enroll. The course content is essentially that of a music education pedagogy class, requiring students to learn theoretical concepts such as the CORE standards in music, children's cognitive and emotional musical development, assessment and observation techniques, practical teaching strategies, and lesson planning. Lesson plans and in-class teaching demonstrations help students implement music-oriented teaching approaches (Kodaly, Orff, Dalcroze), use concepts centered on music elements, and focus on proper singing. As they are interdisciplinary arts majors, they also learn the theories, principles, and application of arts integration. Although this may seem to be an already-encumbered curriculum, the distance between PBL and arts integration is not as far as one might think. In Chapter 2, for example, Merryl Goldberg discusses arts integration in relation to PBL in which she cites educational philosophers whose work is rooted in learning by doing – an approach which is at the heart of PBL. Since pedagogy classes are essentially "hands-on" in nature, I believed I would have to alter very few fundamental elements to create a successful PBL that would bring a new dimension to the course.

Implementation

For purposes of comparison, I decided to implement the PBL in this course twice – once each in the fall of both 2016 and 2017, albeit with changes in the PBL for the second implementation. Since it was a pedagogy class, I felt that students should have some background in PBL so that they might also be able to use the process in their own classrooms. After doing a bit of research, I found, to my surprise, that PBL is a very familiar approach to teaching in K–12 classroom settings as well as in the college classroom. In fact, unlike higher education, PBLs are far more commonly found in the K–12 setting. Although often a bit more fundamental in their scope and approach, K–12 PBL lesson plans are available on numerous websites, with subjects ranging from math, to science, to social studies, and to all of the arts. The Buck Institute for Education (bie.org), for example, has made PBL a priority for preparing students for a successful life and offers a plethora of material including blogs, webinars, handouts, and curriculum planning. The website Edutopia.org, supported by George Lucas Education Foundation, also has numerous resources on PBLs for the K–12 classroom, including articles on starting, pitfalls, ideas, etc. PBL for K–12 schools is so popular that even school furniture supply companies such as School Outfitters provide website materials, equipment, articles, and other information on PBL. PBL is seen as an alternative and progressive learning strategy that goes hand in hand with other models such as the Flipped Classroom, Blended Learning, and Teacher-led Project work. With this background in mind, I began development of my PBL.

The class size for Music and the Child is small, with approximately 12 students enrolled each semester. The small group atmosphere lends itself to group work and energetic discussions quite well. Another positive is that the AFC program is based on interdisciplinary, hands-on learning, which means that students are very used to leading other groups, peer-practice teaching, and participating in and organizing group projects that result in some type of performance (theater, dance, music) or product (lesson plans, art work). Implementing a project such as this was absolutely de rigueur for these students and should be relatively easy – or so I thought. Although the number of complaints regarding the existence of a group project in the curriculum was considerably fewer than in other classes reported by my colleagues, the nature of the project itself was a bit more involved than what AFC students were initially comfortable with. As it turns out, AFC students' familiarity with hands-on learning did not necessarily prepare them for the level of independence the project entailed, or the level of responsibility required for managing their time and gauging their progression throughout the process. In anticipation of this, I created a very thorough network of drop boxes for each stage of the project (see below).

Case Study #1

To make better use of time in the curriculum, I decided to revamp an original teaching experience put in place several years earlier and convert it into the PBL. In 2014, I created an external teaching component to the class, where students would individually develop their own lesson plan based on the course material and teach it in an actual classroom. The College at Brockport is fortunate to have a Child Development Center located on campus, which used to serve as a teaching lab for education majors. In this initial "pre-PBL" course curriculum, I asked students to pair up (three if there were an odd number of students in the class). Students then wrote their own individual 15-minute music lesson plan, consisting of a warm-up and a song with a game or movement of some kind. The pair would teach back-to-back, for a total of 30 minutes of teaching. I would then give each student feedback on their teaching and ask them for a reflection.

In the fall of 2015, I received a classroom grant to promote civic learning and student engagement. The grant provided up to $500 to buy instruments, books, CDs, etc. related to promoting civic learning and responsibility among preschoolers. The following fall (2016), when the opportunity to construct a PBL came along, the presence of an outside parameter – that of civic and social responsibility – seemed like the perfect context in which to implement the PBL as it invited a curriculum that married music with civic learning in a preschool classroom.

This is where my first attempt at a PBL quickly ran into a problem. As I designed the PBL, I realized that there was little I could do to make this completely problem-based given all of the restrictions I had. Because I had established a relationship with the school's childcare center in which my students would teach music lessons at least once a week, we were limited in terms of the final form of the project. Like several other colleagues, I opted for a more "project-based" approach, in which the outcome was fixed, requiring students to teach a lesson in a classroom. The project still had real-world implications, however, in that they had to solve the issue of *how* this was to be taught.

My problem/project question became: How might you use music to convey social and civic responsibility to preschoolers? In the first fall semester implementation, I limited students to creating integrated lessons of one half-hour each, whereas in the second implementation a year later, I left the final product up to the groups, hoping for more diverse and creative approaches to solve the problem.

As it was a pedagogy course, I introduced the differentiation between Project- and Problem-based Learning to the class as well, and as I elaborated in the introduction of this book, they are both similar with the exception of the final outcome: Project-based Learning requires the creation of a product or performance, whereas Problem-based final outcomes may be concrete or in the form of a proposed solution or presentation (Table 11.1).

Development of Group Project into PBL

The processes and procedures for this required students to take responsibility, albeit what I would call "guided" or "scaffolded" responsibility. In actuality,

Table 11.1 Comparison Chart of PBL Implementation 2014–17

Pedagogical and Concept Elements Required	2014 Regular Course	2015 Civic Responsibility Grant Rec'd	2016 PBL	2017 PBL
Group work	Pairs (2–3)	Small groups (3–4)	Small groups (3–4)	Small groups (3–4)
Music concept in lesson plan	yes	yes	yes	yes
Extra-musical concept of civic responsibility in lesson plan	no	yes	yes	yes
Pedagogical input/alterations from instructor	Regular music lesson plan instruction	Additional music lesson plus integrated lesson plan instruction	Additional pre-project guidance/scaffolding plus regular and integrated lesson plan instruction	Additional pre-project guidance/scaffolding plus regular and integrated lesson plan instruction
Teaching reflection	yes	yes	yes	yes
PBL reflection			yes	yes
Instructor workload	Minimal	Moderate	High (pre- and post-project)	Moderate
Student workload	Minimal	Moderate	High	Moderate
			Eight classroom contact hours required	Two classroom contact hours required

my approach falls more in line with Vygotsky's "Zone of Proximal Development" rather than scaffolding, in that I set out a range of tasks for students to complete with help and guidance rather than demonstrating and having them complete the tasks independently.

Overall, *the project had three distinct stages*:

A) **Pre-Project Planning**: Establish relationship with external site (in this case, the campus childcare center), including meeting with director, cooperating teachers, and scheduling setup
B) **PBL Development and Implementation**: Over the course of five weeks, students were to observe four classes, brainstorm, create, and then teach their lessons
C) **Reflection**: Write reflection on the group project as well as their individual lesson.

Pre-Project Planning: Although I had already established this project by discussing it at length with the director of the campus childcare center, I felt that students needed to gain a modicum of real-world experience and take responsibility by directly connecting with the center themselves to set up their schedules. Working with an external institution such as the childcare center meant that students had to adhere to the needs of the institution rather than their own. Not only did students have the usual issues with when they could meet with their group, but they also had to coordinate their schedules with the childcare center, which is highly regulated by the state (lunch, nap, snack, playtime).

Students completed all of these tasks and also met with the cooperating teachers to find out if any students had special needs of any kind, or IEPs or pullouts. One group encountered two students being pulled out for speech therapy as well as other special needs instruction. One student wrote,

We were informed that one of the students does have a hard time focusing and she is sometimes at BOCES (board of cooperative educational services) depending on the day. So they gave us some class cues to use in order to get her attention if she gets off track.

The most difficult task of all concerned the project timeline and goals. Whether it was due to the juggling of so many already-packed schedules or a lack of full understanding of the project or work entailed, students did not develop reasonable timelines for what they needed to do and by when they needed to do it. I gave them the completion deadlines for all activities, but as far as their own work, they were not able to organize or visualize their rate of progress. Ultimately, the teaching school deadline was enough of a major incentive that the tasks were all completed on time, but not without difficulty.

Table 11.2 PBL Dropbox Examples

Project Dropboxes (each with a hard deadline)

    I. Pre-project Planning

        A. Meetings
        B. Project Timelines and Goals

    II. PBL Development and Implementation

        A. Brainstorming
        B. Lesson Planning
        C. Observation write-up (4 hours)
        D. Teaching lessons

   III. Reflection

        A. Individual Reflection on PBL and on teaching
        B. Group Reflection on PBL and teaching

To ensure that students were on task, I set up drop boxes for each of these stages, in which the group as a whole could submit work rather than each individual member of the group (Table 11.2).

Brainstorming: To fulfill the civic responsibility component of the lesson, I devoted an entire class session to helping them develop a topic for their group and encouraged them to work outside of class as well. In-class brainstorming activities included a "round-robin" game, where students arranged in their groups of four, each wrote down a vocabulary word related to civic responsibility on a paper. They then passed the paper to their right, where that new person would then contribute a word related to the previous word written front of them, and so on. By the end, the original word had developed into a large network of vocabulary organically inspired in a creative and fun way.

Civic Responsibility Topics included:

1. Recycling/Environment
2. Emotions
3. Self-care
4. Manners
5. Safety
6. Respect
7. Sharing
8. Kindness
9. Cleanliness
10. Good behavior

Each group was responsible for developing four lessons centered around a topic of civic responsibility, with each student writing and lead teaching a full 30-minute lesson. In addition, the lessons must be integrated, including music (usually a song and movement or game) and music concepts, as well as other arts integration activities. Students could elect to include any of the other art forms, but including music was required (e.g. visual art, literature, and/or drama/theater).

Examples: Group 1. Manners, Safety, Respect, Sharing
            Group 2. Recycling, Being a Good Friend, Emotions, Self-Care

Music Concepts included (examples):

1. Tempo
2. Dynamics
3. Rhythm
4. Beat
5. Timbre

Integrated Aspects

Student creativity extended to all aspects of the lesson, from movement to literature to theater. Excellent examples of music included having student compose their own songs just for the PBL or adapting lyrics to a known melody. Inclusion of children's literature ("The Rainbow Fish," "The Curvy Tree") demonstrated very nuanced and detailed thought as students guided children through the narrative's metaphoric meanings to address common behavior (e.g. the significance of being different, following the "golden rule," treating people with respect). Students even incorporated sounds and rhythms as leitmotifs when certain words were mentioned. One theatrical skit involved the student acting out different types of moral scenarios involving stealing, lying, etc., after which students had to decide the correct action should be in the morally ambiguous situations (e.g. what to do if someone leaves their purse behind (keep it or try to return it)). For movement, one student had children place recyclable objects into the proper bins during a game. Overall, the lessons were incredibly cohesive, well-thought-out, and successful.

Analysis of Case Study #1 Implementation

In retrospect, this first implementation went extremely well. Group projects were well-thought-out, and each lesson plan was enhanced and made coherent, stable, and relevant by input from other members of the group. In other words, everyone had input into each other's final lesson, making sure that it kept up to the standards of the entire group and fit with the goals of the lesson.

The depth of understanding regarding the PBL and their teaching in general was apparent in their reflections, lesson plans, and in the amount of time that the groups were expected to be together and observe each other's teaching.
Student Group Reflection Excerpt, Fall 2016

Corinne's lesson was wonderful. Her enthusiasm carried over to the children who in return engaged in all the activities she had present. Her presentation included songs and a story about recycling. The game was a recycling sorting race. The children had fun putting the items into the bins, but were a little too overzealous to understand the sorting concept. The children then used their recyclables as instruments to jam along to Corinne's song. She ended the lesson by reviewing what a landfill was and why it is important to recycle. Overall, the lesson was conducive to the topic of civil responsibility. The children had grasped the concept and enjoyed singing along to the music. Justine's lesson focused on the care of others and the importance of making friends. Her song was "Make New Friends" which she sang both by herself and with the children. The activity included having the children stand in a circle and dance around while they all sang. The lesson was conducted appropriately for their age and truly expressed the message it had intended to give. Ali's lesson followed all of the criteria and included musical elements which the kids thoroughly enjoyed.

Case Study #2

For the second implementation, I decided to alter the assignment dramatically. I reduced the number of drop boxes and step-by-step instructions, and I reduced the length of time students would spend in the classroom both in an observational and teaching capacity. I *suggested* four observations, instead of *requiring* four. The immediate impact of these changes manifested almost immediately, with groups deciding that two observations were enough for them to get a sense of the classroom, teachers, and students rather than four. In terms of their teaching hours, instead of all of them appearing as a group and watching others teach their lesson (requiring all of them to be present for four hours watching each other teach), I required only one final lesson on the topic of civic responsibility, with all four of them cooperatively teaching. My rationale was that this would encourage students to work together even more closely to brainstorm, develop, and implement the lesson. The format of the lesson was left open, without any specific indication of interdisciplinarity – only the civic responsibility topic along with music integration.

Analysis for Case Study #2

Interestingly, the results of this revised PBL ranged from excellent to less than stellar, suggesting an increased volatility in the outcomes. In fact, one of the groups' presented projects represented the best lesson I had ever witnessed, while the group that taught before them was easily the worst. Compared to the first year of implementation which resulted in more balanced, stable, and creative final lessons, this year's erratic results lead me to believe that there were not enough guidelines for them to follow, and some students were completely lost.

One positive was that students complained far less about scheduling problems in 2017, but this was due to the reduced number of required trips to the childcare classroom for both observations and teaching. The reduction in classroom hours between the two semesters was dramatic – from eight hours in the 2016 PBL to less than two hours in the 2017 implementation.

Final topics included germs and cleanliness (washing hands), kindness, and helping others. The least successful group was highly unorganized, not at all self-reflective, and did not create an integrated lesson using music and civic responsibility. Below is a reflection from the most successful group, which was organized to the point of precision, and who had clearly rehearsed their lesson plans out loud a number of times resulting in a smooth performance.

Student Group Reflection #1 (excerpt)

One thing that I really think worked was the order of steps we went in. We first introduced the topic, then taught the song, then taught the hand movements, taught the beat, and then finally we added instruments. It was very important that we got the students practicing the beat before they got instruments in their hands because then they had some type of prior experience with what the directions were once they had instruments. Since young children can be very eager to make noise, it's important to make sure they know what they should be doing before adding something like instruments to distract their attention from their teacher. Counting to eight to start singing once we added the beat was very helpful in making sure everyone was on the same page too. It was also really good that our song was very simple. At first, we were worried that our song was too simple, but it turned out to be a good thing because we were able to easily teach the song and then do several different activities with the song once the children learned it. One last thing that was really strong about our lesson was that we broke the students up into groups. These groups were good for several reasons. For one, it helped us manage the children better once they had their instruments. Students were given more individual attention with their group leaders and so it was easier to keep them on task. Another thing that was good as that in these groups, we all mentioned to the children that we would be having a contest. This is very important because by introducing a competition, it really motivated the students to do their best work in the hopes of winning. Lastly, since there were three different instrument groups we were working with, it made sense to break them up so the classroom noises would be less jumbled.

The following observation is from one of the groups in the middle of the range.

Student Group Reflection #2 (excerpt)

These activities served to accomplish the PBL assignment because they taught the children kindness and helping behaviors across activities through the incorporation of music and instruments. The three sections allowed for children to first become acquainted with the lesson topic and then apply it in subsequent sections. This demonstrated that the children truly understood the content of the lesson, because they not only recognized kind and helpful behaviors during the warm-up activity, but could also identify and explain them across multiple situations and contexts (i.e., story and rhyme).

Several factors became immediately apparent concerning the structural formatting of the PBLs. My decision to reduce the "scaffolding" or "infrastructure" for the PBL did not work as planned. Instead, students became *less* engaged rather than more, and students fell into what I would refer to as "typical group work mode" which involved one student carrying on the bulk of the work for the rest of the group.
One student commented,

In terms of what could have been improved, I think that the group could have been more prepared as a whole. Even though the nature of the project required ample amounts of collaboration, I received little help on the development of the lesson plan and produced most (if not all) of the ideas on my own. Although several attempts were made to meet as a group, group members were often too busy or would bail on these arrangements. As a result of not contributing, other group members were nervous during the presentation, reading directly off of their scripts and making poor transitions that could have been remedied with further preparation or increased familiarity. In critique of my own performance, I was nervous because we were only able to practice the lesson the day of the presentation. During the lesson, I was flushed because of this anticipatory anxiety, however, I know this could have been remedied with more practice. Despite these shortcomings, I believe that the presentation was successful, and I was relieved that the other group members both appreciated the lesson plan and learned the material rather efficiently.

Such results are not desired nor are they educationally sound. Rushing at the last minute to learn a lesson plan or practice, it does not make for a good educational experience for either the student teacher or the student. The excellent results from 2016 demonstrate that the additional hours of observation and teaching paid off substantially for everyone involved, and gave the PBL process time enough to work.

Assessment

Students were assessed based on several dimensions, such as self-reflection, peer assessment, assignment completion including the lesson plan, and final outcome of the presentation (in this case, their teaching). I observed each of the students teaching their lesson and provided individual feedback on their teaching. They were then required to fill out a reflection of their own teaching, and an additional reflection on the lesson for each member of their group. One final reflection concerned the PBL as a whole, and their thoughts on its development, implementation, and their levels of engagement with the project and its failure or success.

Conclusion

Given the parameters of the class curricula, the project took on a more education-related identity, incorporating observations and teaching, widening the classroom teaching and learning experience in a very hands-on and concrete way. It requires students to think beyond the walls of the classroom and work cooperatively with others to achieve an agreed-upon goal, adapting activities and behaviors which occur "in the real world" every day. The usefulness of such an approach in a teaching classroom is even more profound since it is a teaching and learning strategy with a great deal of support from K–12 school systems vying to include 21st-century learning practices in their classrooms.

Problem-based versus Project-based Learning are often confused and misunderstood. As mentioned earlier, the main difference concerns the final product of the learning and not the process. Both encourage real-world applications, whereas Problem-based is more flexible in the possible of final formatting. I plan on implementing the PBL in this course again next fall, but reverting back to the original model with the increased monitoring along each step of the way.

Bibliography

Vygotsky, L. *Mind in Society: Development of Higher Psychological Processes*. Cambridge, MA: Harvard University Press, 1978.

12

Using Problem-Based Learning to Address Behavior and Curricular Issues in the Self-Contained Music Classroom

TRACY S. WANAMAKER

In the second chapter concerning education, Tracy brings us into two Special Education Music courses and their Problem-based Learnings. Once again, courses that have state mandates, such as education classes, are much more restricted in the flexibility of their curriculum. Tracy demonstrates, through two detailed PBL approaches, the process of helping students develop strategies to teach music in the special education classroom, from behavior management for students with disabilities to curricular design for including music in the high school. In the end, Tracy shares student work and assesses the impact of the PBL on her class.

~

Bachelor-Level Music Education degree programs are designed to prepare future music educators with the skills and knowledge to successfully teach music in K–12 schools. Because these future educators will also be dealing with the same types of engagement issues with their own students that we do in the collegiate classroom, it is critical that we teach them the skills that they need to be able to problem-solve in their teaching. Problem-based Learning (PBL) is the perfect platform to do this.

As a specialist in Music Education for students with disabilities, I wanted to design projects for my undergraduates that dealt with the most common challenges that they will face when working with students with disabilities and the types of problems that they would most likely encounter in their own classrooms. Through years of research and discussion with current educators, I have discovered that the two areas that most public school teachers report difficulties in when working with students with disabilities are classroom management and curricular design for students in self-contained classrooms. Using these two concerns, I developed PBL questions for two of my undergraduate music classes to research.

158 • Tracy S. Wanamaker

**Problem 1: Effective Classroom Management Techniques
for Students with Disabilities**

In New York State, all future educators must take a three-credit introductory
class concerning working with students with disabilities. At the Crane School
of Music, we fulfill this requirement with MUCE 445 "Music in Special Education," an upper division required music education course, which is typically
taken in the student's junior or senior year shortly before their student teaching practicum. Each semester, there are typically two sections of this class offered with an average class size of 12–16 students per section. This class meets
three times a week for 50-minute class sessions.

Music in Special Education is designed to acquaint music education students with the individualized education program (IEP) process, music materials and techniques for teaching students with disabilities in inclusive
music classes. The student learning outcomes (SLOs) for the class are as
follows:

1. Develop an understanding of the role of music education for students
   with disabilities
2. Become familiar with the primary laws pertaining to special
   education
3. Develop an understanding of the characteristics of each disability
   included in the special education laws
4. Develop knowledge of and practice classroom teaching techniques
   and behavior management strategies for the inclusive music classroom as well as the self-contained classroom
5. Develop knowledge of adaptive materials and resources for the inclusive music classroom.

The PBL Project

I chose to design a PBL experience for Music in Special Education because
developing knowledge of classroom management strategies and techniques is
already one of the stated learning objectives of this course. Instead of lecturing about the many different behavior management strategies and systems, I
felt that the students would develop a deeper understanding of what strategies
might work for them personally if they explored strategies that they had seen
in action, and then narrowed down their research to a specific idea that they
wanted to research in more depth.

Many pre-service teachers view classroom management as a set of disciplinary tactics that a teacher takes in the classroom as a result of "bad" behavior. Often, these responses only consider the behavior itself and don't take
into consideration the antecedents and consequences of the behavior. When
working with students with disabilities, it is crucial to understand that often
these behaviors are a result of the disability instead of the child misbehaving.

Each behavior must be examined, and specific behavior management strategies must be applied based on the specific reason for the behavior instead of simply punishing a student that may not understand why they are being punished. To help students understand the types of behavior management strategies available to them in the classroom and the effective ways to use them, I developed the problem for this PBL project:

> What are behavior management strategies that a teacher can use to effectively address behavior issues in the music classroom, taking into account the student's disability and their reasons for participating in the problem behavior (antecedents/consequences)?

The SLOs for this project included:

1. Develop an understanding of how to determine if a behavior is a "problem behavior" in the classroom
2. Develop the ability to access the antecedents and consequences of a "problem behavior" in the classroom
3. Develop an understanding of possible strategies that could be used to address identified problem behaviors and how to use these strategies effectively
4. Create resource materials to utilize and to refer to as needed outlining how to use specific behavior management strategies effectively.

To approach this problem, the students were divided into groups of three or four (depending on their class section size) to do their research. These groupings were done randomly because in real-world situations, teachers often collaborate with other teachers and professionals concerning specific student behavior issues to ensure continuity, and often these other professionals may not have the same thoughts about specific techniques. By working in groups where there were often differing opinions, it gave the students a chance to practice the communication skills needed to come to a consensus on if and how a specific strategy should be implemented.

First, we discussed as a class the characteristics of students with disabilities that often have behavior problems in inclusive classroom settings, including students with specific behavior disorders, autism, learning disabilities, and ADHD. Then, the groups were asked to collect information from their own observations and research concerning possible behavior management strategies using the following initial set of questions:

> What types of behavior management strategies have you observed teachers using in the music classroom? What types of behavior do you feel that the teacher was addressing? Do you feel that these strategies were effective? Why or why not?

The students were given a week to conduct their research, including approximately an hour and a half of class time.

At the end of the week, students reported their research findings. Each group was asked to describe the strategies that they thought would be most effective to address the most common behavioral issues. These were then compiled in a list form where all students could access them. Once each strategy was described and all groups had presented, the class took this list and grouped strategies into the four following categories of behavior strategies: Antecedent Techniques (Classroom rules, routines, seating arrangements, etc.), Behavior Systems/Techniques (Token Reward Systems, Time Out, Extinction, etc.), Punitive Actions (Reprimand, Suspension, Notes to parents, etc.), and Cultural Differences in Behavior. While "cultural differences in behavior" is not exactly a "strategy," it was determined that this was an important research area because many students participate in certain behaviors because in their culture, they are accepted behaviors, but they may be perceived by the teacher as problem behaviors in the classroom.

Each group was then asked to choose a topic from this list to research in more depth. They were allowed to choose a broad topic (such as antecedent techniques) or a behavior system to research. Each semester, the students involved decided to research varying topics, but over the three semesters that this problem was presented, these were the topics the groups chose to research:

- Antecedent Techniques
- Token Reward Systems
- Cultural Differences in Behavior
- Extinction
- Time Out
- Reprimand

Once they had determined which topic they wanted to research, they were given the following directions:

You will present your research findings to the class in an 8 to 10-minute presentation. Your presentation should include information on how to use your chosen technique effectively in the classroom and should include any 'Do's and Don'ts' that a teacher should be aware of when using this strategy. You should also include information on when you feel that this strategy should be utilized in the classroom and the types of behaviors that you feel could be addressed with this technique.

As part of your presentation, you should give the class a 'product' containing key points of your research for future reference. This can be an interactive PowerPoint (with audio and/or video), a brochure with graphics, or other 'product' as approved by the instructor. This product should be more than just a typical handout or PowerPoint.

The students were again given a week to perform their research and prepare their presentations and products. While all groups did prepare a handout or PowerPoint to disseminate their research, they all added another component to emphasis how to use the technique effectively in the classroom. These additional components included instructional videos, brochures, and Google databases for the class to reference, add to, and use in the future role-plays and demonstrations.

PBL Reflection

The student response to this project has been favorable overall. They reported that they enjoyed the interactive components of each other's research and found the demonstrations most helpful when learning about a specific technique. As always with group projects, several students reported that they felt that some students had done more work than others. This was obvious to me based on their participation levels in the culminating presentations.

As the instructor, I found that this PBL experience worked well for most of the students in the classroom. The initial questions generated good classroom discussion about different techniques and how they should be implemented, and overall, the students involved came away with a better understanding of how these techniques could be used in a positive manner.

During the first semester that I presented this problem, I did encounter bias issues toward some of the behavior management techniques based on the students' previous observations and experiences and found it difficult to guide their initial negative perceptions to more positive ideas without giving them more direct instruction on how to use certain techniques. For example, many pre-service teachers view "time out" as a punishment, but when it is used effectively, it is used as a chance for the student to remove themselves from an overwhelming situation and calm down. If the class had a negative bias toward "time out," it was easy for them to find documentation supporting their argument that it should not be used, but in reality, the ability to remove yourself and calm down in a stressful situation (which is what "time out" is supposed to teach) is an important skill for all of us to learn to utilize but is a crucial skill to develop for a student with autism. To deal with this issue, I lengthened the initial questions to include which types of behaviors the teacher was trying to address, so that we could examine as a class, the different strategies could be used to positively change behavior over the long term instead of letting students stick to a specific bias and discard a system that might be beneficial for future classroom management.

I have completed this PBL project over three semesters with six different classes and have been dismayed by the wide disparity of the research completed by the different groups. Because the research is very self-directed, some groups search out multiple resources including varying opinions about how their technique should be utilized, whereas other groups only find enough information to fulfill the basic requirements of the project, without searching any further. This has made me consider adding a requirement to use a specific minimum number of resources for their final presentation. When I do this project again, I may implement this to determine if it deepens their understanding of the technique and improves the quality of the information they present to their peers in the culminating project.

One of the major challenges of group work concerns work distribution and equitable participation. This has been particularly difficult in this specific project because of the difficulty assigning specific roles or dividing subject matter so that group members can individually research specific aspects of a technique. After feedback from some students that other group members had not participated fully in the project, I am considering adding an individual participation grade as part of their final project grade to encourage more participation by all group members. This grade would be determined by anonymous feedback given on group participation by the group members and would be collected after the project was complete – the anonymity allowing students to feel comfortable enough to provide honest feedback.

Overall, this project has helped students explore classroom management techniques in more depth than they would have otherwise. It also provided each class additional resources that they could refer to in the future when implementing these strategies. I do plan to continue using this PBL project with future classes utilizing some of the changes discussed above.

Problem 2: Designing a Music Curriculum for a Self-Contained High School Music Class

For most students with disabilities, inclusion is the educational goal. When students are educated using an inclusion model, they spend all of their school day in the general education classroom, including the music classroom. While a majority of students with disabilities can be successful in an inclusive music education setting if the proper supports are provided, some students do not have the ability to sing in a choir or play an instrument in a traditional ensemble. Most music educators struggle with this aspect of curricular planning, as they're unsure of how to accommodate the students while providing a music curriculum that is both relevant and cognizant of these students' educational needs. According to Bassett and Cullen (2011),

> Access to mainstream is an absolute right of students with disabilities but the issue of appropriateness seems to have gotten lost in the shuffle…it is

necessary to ask the question where does the student do his or her best learning...if the answer is that the student learns best in a less complex, specialized environment, in which there are fewer students, fewer distractions, and many more opportunities to learn and practice the skills they will need to be successful, then that is the least restrictive environment in which the student can receive an appropriate public education.[1]

In other words, students with more severe disabilities deserve a music class that is geared toward their abilities and needs, and often this means that they need to be educated in a modified or self-contained setting where their individual needs can be met. The question of how to accomplish this is a consistent topic in my discussions with seasoned music educators. In the elementary classroom, most music educators find they can adapt their current curriculum for these students, but for high school-aged students in life skills classes, this becomes more of a challenge. They don't feel that they have the skills necessary to develop a music curriculum that is relevant for high school students in a life skills program. Therefore, I developed my PBL project question:

> How do you develop a music curriculum for the self-contained high school classroom that is engaging, effectual, addresses the common core music standards and is age-appropriate?

At SUNY Potsdam, we offer a course that is the perfect venue for exploring this question. MUCE 447 – Strategies for Teaching Music in the Self-Contained Classroom is an upper-division music education elective (MUCE) and is a required course for students enrolled in the Music in Special Education Concentration at the Crane School of Music. This class is offered every semester and usually contains 4–8 students. Students typically take it the semester before they student teach. This class meets three times a week for 50-minute class sessions.

Strategies for Teaching Music in the Self-Contained Special Education Classroom is designed to acquaint music education students with planning music goals, objectives, and activities in self-contained special education programs for children with a variety of disabilities including intellectual disabilities, physical handicaps, autism, behavior disorders, learning disabilities, speech impairments, and multiple disabilities. Adaptation of standard materials and techniques and creation of originally designed materials to use to teach music skills and concepts are discussed. The SLOs for the class are as follows:

1. Develop an understanding of the role of music education for students with special learning needs
2. Develop an understanding of a variety of disabilities and the challenges that these disabilities may cause students in the music classroom

3. Develop ability to assess each student's skills and use this assessment to set appropriate goals and objectives in a classroom situation
4. Develop knowledge of and practice classroom techniques and strategies for the self-contained classroom
5. Develop knowledge of adaptive materials and resources to use in the self-contained music classroom

The reason that I chose this class for the project is because it focuses on discussing and developing strategies for teaching music in a self-contained special education classroom. Additionally, there is very little research in this area, so students must develop their own ideas and thoughts about this topic, which creates the perfect environment to implement a PBL project.

The students were ultimately assigned to develop a 12-lesson curriculum for a high school-level life skills class that addressed this problem. While the ultimate outcome was a project, this was addressed in a problem-solving format, so it is what I would describe as a hybrid Problem-/Project-based learning format. While the students were using problem-solving techniques throughout the entire process, it was necessary to develop a final project as an outcome to this problem so that they could apply the information that they had gathered.

The student learning objectives for this project were as follows:

1. Develop an understanding of the role of music education for high school-aged students with special learning needs that are in a life skills program
2. Develop an understanding of a variety of disabilities and the challenges that these disabilities may cause students in the music classroom
3. Develop ability to assess each student's skills and use this assessment to set appropriate goals and objectives in a classroom situation
4. Develop knowledge of adaptive materials and resources to use in the self-contained music classroom.

The project was initially designed to be implemented over 12 weeks during the 15-week spring of 2016 semester. Because it was well received during the first implementation, it has been repeated for the subsequent three semesters. Each semester, the class is split into three- to four-member groups depending on the class size that semester to work on the problem.

Because this is a complicated problem, the process was broken into five sections that were addressed over a 12-week period during the semester. The students were given a question to research every two weeks. At the end of each two-week period, the groups reported to each other on their findings and then received the next question. To share information with each other and with the class, sharing forums were created on Moodle (SUNY Potsdam's learning platform) where students could add information that they wanted to share. When working in groups, many groups used Google Docs to gather, organize, and present material as they worked through each problem.

The first four biweekly questions addressed the following issues and resulting questions:

Question 1: Common Core Music Standards

How do you effectively meet the common core music standards when working with students with multiple disabilities?

This question was addressed first because this is where all curricular planning should start. The 2014 Common Core Music Standards[2] were created by the National Coalition of Core Arts Standards in response to the national Common Core Standards. These standards are broken into four artistic processes that all students should be participating in while in the music classroom: Creating, Performing, Responding, and Connecting to music. But how do we include students that may not be able to sing, play traditional instruments, or respond verbally or in writing? For this question, students spent time researching the standards and compiling lists of ideas and possible solutions. These are some of the possible solutions that were compiled during their research:

1. Creating:
   - Composition and improvisation using pentatonic scales or color systems
   - Creating musical maps or nontraditional notation to create scores
   - Using hand signs to create melodic lines
   - Soundscaping books and video clips
   - Using music apps to create compositions
2. Performing:
   - Using adapted instruments for students with physical impairments
   - Using communication devices for singing
   - Using a device such as Soundbeam that allows students to participate by making musical choices that are then played electronically
   - Use movement within a performance for students to respond to the music
3. Responding:
   - Responding to music using movement aides such as scarves or streamers
   - Creating listening and contour maps
   - Recreating musical ideas using classroom instruments

- Musical drawing activities
- Using emojis and word lists to help describe music
- Sharing favorite songs or pieces and explain why the student likes it
- Comparing performances of select pieces
4. Connecting:
  - Songwriting about topics that the student is interested in
  - Analyzing song lyrics
  - Discussions about where we listen to music and the types of music we might listen to in different environments
  - Practicing audience etiquette in different venues and contexts
  - Comparing different styles of music from a variety of genres, cultures, and historical periods
  - Create playlists for future listening.

Question 2: Modalities

How do you structure lessons to ensure that all modalities are engaged and multiple intelligences are considered?

Most teachers are aware of Barbe's theory that there are three predominant learning modalities – visual, auditory, and kinesthetic modes[3] – and agree that student's modality strengths should be considered in instructional planning. In my experience, teachers often overlook Gardner's Theories of Multiple Intelligences (1983)[4] that identifies eight different "intelligences" and suggests that these should also be considered in instructional planning. According to this theory,

> we are all able to know the world through language, logical-mathematical analysis, spatial representation, musical thinking, the use of the body to solve problems or to make things, an understanding of other individuals, and an understanding of ourselves. Where individuals differ is in the strength of these intelligences - the so-called profile of intelligences -and in the ways in which such intelligences are invoked and combined to carry out different tasks, solve diverse problems, and progress in various domains.[5]

In other words, we all learn in a variety of different ways and will have different strengths and weaknesses in the classroom. Gardner goes on to suggest that "The broad spectrum of students - and perhaps the society as a whole - would be better served if disciplines could be presented in a number of ways and learning could be assessed through a variety of means." When working with students with disabilities whose strengths and weaknesses may be more pronounced, making sure that we present information in a number of ways in the classroom becomes crucial in our curricular planning.

When students were asked to research this question, they again compiled a list of strategies that could be used in their final project based on the different learning modalities and intelligences. These ideas included:

1. **Visual-Spatial (includes Visual Modality):**
   - Draw/write on a board
   - Project visuals
   - Give students listening maps (or have them create their own)
   - Use graphic notation
   - Provide sheet music for students who can read traditional notation
   - Model/demonstrate what you want students to do on their instruments or with their bodies
   - Watch videos that go along with music
   - Have students observe each other visually and give feedback
   - Use picture/words cards, books, puppets, and other materials that provide visual representations of songs
   - Have students create visual art based off of songs and music
   - Have students compose music based off of visual art
2. **Verbal-Linguistic (includes both visual and auditory modalities):**
   - Engage the student in conversation about the subject matter
   - Ask verbal questions about the material
   - Ask for oral summaries of material
   - Repeat verbal instructions
   - Read material aloud to them
   - Use videos with audio clips
   - Learn music by rote
   - Demonstrate instruments before playing it with class
   - Have them put material to a rhythm or tune and rehearse it aloud
3. **Bodily – Kinesthetic/Tactile:**
   - Follow listening and contour maps with a finger
   - Use some form of body movement (snapping fingers, pacing, mouthing ideas) while reciting material to be learned
   - Use musical rhythms for memorization patterns
   - Incorporate movement in every lesson in at least one of the activities
   - Hands-on activities such as playing instruments, singing, and moving around
   - Warm-ups involving stretching
   - Learn movements that go along with a song
   - Play instruments (drum circle, boomwhackers, Orff instruments, etc.)
   - Singing games that involve moving around the classroom
   - Learning choreography from a video or musical

- Dancing and moving around to a piece of music
- Body percussion: clapping, tapping, and stomping
- Create movements to a song or a piece of music using scarves, body movements, etc.

4. **Mathematical/Logical:**
   - Sing songs that include counting or simple math in them like Five Little Ducklings (or pumpkins or monkeys)
   - Ask students to count or notice numbers in music (How many sections are in this song? How many times do we sing the chorus? How many different notes do we use in this song?)
   - Discuss mathematical relationships between rhythms and note values
   - Have students count rhythms

5. **Musical:**
   - Singing directions to students
   - Use instruments/songs while learning topics
   - Incorporate all kinds of sounds (musical, environmental, etc.)
   - Create a musical to cover a topic
   - Incorporate other means of music (body percussion,
   - Have background music on while working
   - Analyze music (lyrics, mood, emotions, timbre, etc.)
   - Move to music
   - Incorporate music history in general social studies

6. **Interpersonal:**
   - Group activities like drum circles that don't single them out
   - Give them classroom duties
   - Songs about expressing emotion
   - Let them create music about themselves and their feelings

7. **Intrapersonal:**
   - Work in groups/partners
   - Talk out problems with peers
   - Make learning active (not passive) through the ability to teach others a concept
   - Plan cooperative group games
   - Make activities more student centered
   - Provide a rubric for student/partner activities
   - Incorporate assessment into the learning process
   - One-on-one interviews (peer-based, teacher helps facilitate)
   - Incorporating multiculturalism into topics

8. **Naturalist:**
   - Singing songs about nature (Animals, Plants, Weather, Science)
   - Creating compositions based off of various nature themed literature and artwork (poems or haiku, short stories, paintings)

- Field trips to nature centers and museums and have students write songs or composed pieces inspired by their experiences in nature.

Question 3: Age-Appropriate:
How do you structure lessons that are age-appropriate while still ensuring that students can be successful?

When working with high school-aged students with developmental disabilities, teachers find that while they may still be teaching elementary-level concepts, they are working with students that know that they are high schoolers and don't respond well to material that they perceive is childish. Adamek and Darrow (2010) suggest that

> the use of age-appropriate music activities and materials allows students to function in a more normalized environment, an environment that is closer to that of students their same age who do not have disabilities. World music, folk music, traditional music, and classical music are a few examples of music that can span the age ranges.[6]

For this question, students were asked to compile information and ideas concerning what they would need to consider to ensure that the lessons and materials used in their curriculum were age-appropriate. Their ideas included:

- Have the students take a survey in the beginning of the semester to see what genres of music they like and use this list to compile a list of appropriate songs from different genres to use in class projects
- Pop music and Disney songs are usually big hits with this age level but do not assume all students will like these genres
- Students can use simple melodies or pop songs to write their own lyrics for songwriting projects
- Incorporate world music and classical music into lessons
- Choose age-appropriate instruments
- Use iPad composition apps/games to teach certain concepts
- Encourage independence in every part of the lesson because they are capable of being independent and benefit from being able to practice that skill
- Listen to your students and observe how they react to each activity! If they seem bored or annoyed they definitely are not engaged. You can change the lesson to make it more complex and to challenge them
- Delve into deeper specific historical backgrounds/concepts with more focus (can also correlate well with HS history classes)

- Current events can be basis of musical creations – What important current events are appropriate for the classroom, and how can we be creative in expressing solutions, opinions, etc. through music?
- Teach social/cultural dances as part of movement activities that they will use at future social events (weddings, school dances, sports events)
- Be in touch with current trends (different from events → words, songs, dances, etc.) and see if you can incorporate them into your lessons. Students might latch onto foreign concepts faster with something that is familiar to them as a basis
- Having healthy methods of self-expression is crucial at this age (as well as middle school), so getting them to find ways to personalize their assignments or activities will be beneficial.

Question 4: Technology:

Is there technology available that will make the curriculum more accessible and assist students in reaching learning goals?

We know that using technology in the classroom is beneficial for all students, but for students with disabilities, it can create opportunities for learning and participation that they may not have without it. Meyer (2016) states,

> assistive and accessible technology can help students with special needs overcome a wide variety of challenges. Nonverbal students can communicate using augmentative and alternative communication (AAC) technology; students with physical disabilities can take advantage of special keyboards and monitors; and the accessibility features of Apple iPads and Google Apps for Education can help students with learning disabilities or other challenges.[7]

The question then is how do we apply this knowledge in the music classroom?

Students were again asked to compile information and ideas concerning technology that could be used in the music classroom to help their students gain access to the curriculum and participate more fully in lessons and music making. Their most popular ideas included:

- Using appropriate communication devices and systems that the student may already be using and adding terms that are music specific to these devices as needed
- Using adapted instruments including:
  - o Soundbeam – www.soundbeam.co.uk
  - o The Beamz – www.thebeamz.com
  - o Jamboxx – www.jamboxx.com
  - o Artiphon – https://artiphon.com

- o Skoog – http://skoogmusic.com/
- o Makey – Makey – https://makeymakey.com
- o Aumia – http://aumiapp.com/about.php
- Software and Apps:
  - o To Create Music:
    - Thumb Jam – http://thumbjam.com/
    - MorphWiz – www.wizdommusic.com/products/morphwiz. html
    - iMaschine – www.native-instruments.com/en/products/ maschine/maschine-for-ios/imaschine-2/
    - Bloom – create music by simply touching the screen – https:// itunes.apple.com/us/app/bloom/id292792586?mt=8
    - Beatwave – create music by taping – https://itunes.apple.com/ us/app/beatwave/id363718254?mt=8
    - Splice – to find sounds – https://splice.com
    - GarageBand – www.apple.com/mac/garageband/
    - GuitarLab – get strumming with guitar video lessons – http:// theguitarlab.net
    - Real Piano Pro – full 88 key board with realistic sound and key labels – https://itunes.apple.com/us/app/real-piano/id413943804? mt=8
  - o To Practice Music Concepts:
    - Staff Wars – note and staff recognition game – www.themusic interactive.com
    - Blob Chorus – ear training game – https://itunes.apple.com/ us/app/blob-chorus-ear-training/id484567131?mt=8
    - O-Generator – uses popular and world music to teach key music concepts – www.o-generator.com
    - myRhythm – to improve rhythmic skills – https://itunes.apple. com/us/app/myrhythm/id574316971?mt=8
  - o Other Helpful Apps:
    - NotateMe – allows students to take pictures of sheet music and convert it to digital notation – www.neuratron.com/notateme. html
    - SmartMusic – allows for feedback on their performances – www.smartmusic.com
    - forScore – a place to store all sheet music – https://forscore.co
    - onSong – for chord chart management – https://onsongapp.com.

Final Question:

The final section of the project took the information gathered during the first four sections to answer the larger PBL question:

"How do you develop a music curriculum for the self-contained high school classroom that is engaging, effectual, addresses the common core music standards and is age-appropriate?"

Using the information gathered while answering the first four problems, the students created a 12-lesson plan curricular unit designed for high school students in a life skills program that addressed all of these issues.

Each group created their own curriculum and could choose any topic and format that they chose for these lessons. The outcomes were varied and creative and included some of the following:

- Group 1 – This curriculum focused on creating playlists, exploring popular music, and using student's musical preferences to write their own music and create their own compositions using popular programs and apps such as Splice and Garage Band
- Group 2 – This curriculum focused on planning, promoting, and successfully executing a concert. During the lessons, students learn about crew work, finances, public relations, choosing acts, and concert etiquette
- Group 3 – This curriculum focused on musical expression. Over the first four weeks, the students would be asked to create original compositions using instruments to respond to visual artwork, the second four weeks would be spent creating movement and dance that reflected what they were hearing, and the culminating experience would be writing a song that expressed their feelings
- Group 4 – This curriculum focused on music cultures. The curriculum used singing, playing instruments, and dance to explore different musical cultures while reinforcing basic music skills
- Group 5 – This curriculum was based on three of the four musical processes – Responding, Creating, and Performing. During the first four-week unit, students listened to music and responded using instruments, movement, and classroom room discussion. The second unit involved rewriting a song of their choosing and then recording and orchestrating this version into GarageBand. The final unit focused on playing instruments and planning an "informance" to perform for their families and peers.

While all of the final curricula were very different, they all met the goals of the question: they effectively addressed the core curricular standards, they presented the material being taught in multiple ways to accommodate for multiple learning styles, they were age-appropriate, and they incorporated technology when it was appropriate while also being engaging and effectual for high school-aged students with disabilities. Below is an outline of the first group's project including the musical concepts and specific elements that each lesson covered. This outline demonstrates that all of these elements were being considered when they designed their curriculum:

Lesson 1: How music functions as a way of storytelling
   Specific Element(s): Interpreting lyrics
Lesson 2: Pop song form
   Specific Element(s): Exploring familiar songs/songs that the students like, parts of a pop song, elements of pop song form, describing, and responding to music
Lesson 3: Charting form of pop songs and other different forms of songs, replicating those forms in GarageBand using recorded sounds
   Specific Element(s): Learning a little of GarageBand, Responding to/identifying sections of songs
Lesson 4: Creating beats
   Specific Element(s): creating electronic beats, learning parts of a drum set, identifying sounds of a drum set
Lesson 5: Compiling Playlists, comparing/contrasting musical pieces
   Specific Element(s): Exploring music, describing music
Lesson 6: Improvisation
   Specific Element(s): Improvisation of rhythmic patterns using a drum
Lesson 7: Creating patterns and pieces that have a form
   Specific Element(s): Creating different musical patterns, and then using them to create short pieces that have a distinct form.
Lesson 8: Creating beats
   Specific Element(s): creating electronic beats in Splice and then in HTML 5
Lesson 9: Loops in music
   Specific Element(s): Teach students about looping and how to loop in GarageBand
Lesson 10: Using created beats in Soundtrap
   Specific Element(s): looping our created beats and using them in Soundtrap
Lesson 11: Refining a musical composition
   Specific Element(s): Knowing when a piece is ready for performance/to be shared, editing skills in GarageBand
Lesson 12: Refining and presenting a musical composition
   Specific Element(s): Knowing what needs to be refined and fine-tuned before a piece is ready for performance/to be shared, editing skills in GarageBand, saving/exporting their finished work.

PBL Reflection:

Overall, this PBL project was a success. The students responded well to the task and created interesting projects while answering the PBL problem. All of the groups went in very different directions with their final projects which made it interesting for the groups to share with each other, while also demonstrating that there are multiple ways to address these ideas in the classroom.

The student response to the PBL questions, and the final outcome was positive. They stated that by focusing on one question at a time initially, it allowed them to gather the information needed to successfully complete the final project. They responded positively to having the opportunity to develop an entire curricular unit for a class. Many of them had never done this and found that looking at a curricular unit as an entire problem instead of as one lesson developing from the next gave them a much better idea of how to approach the unit and address student needs and learning outcomes in the curriculum design.

The students were to work as groups, but each group quickly fell into a format on their own often resulting in different people in the group researching different parts of each question. While they had to come together to organize and present the information, much of it was gathered on an individual basis. The material that they were researching allowed them to break it into individual components for each group member to research individually, but I found that the more the group members worked individually, the less cohesive the final project tended to be. To handle this, I encouraged them to make sure that all of their information collected for each section was organized before presenting, which seemed to eliminate some of the possible research gaps.

To ensure that all group members were participating in the research, an individual participation grade was included in the final grade for the overall project. This grade was determined by anonymous feedback given on group participation by the group members using an easy-to-use rubric. The rubrics were filled out anonymously and were collected after the project was complete in hopes that students will feel comfortable providing honest feedback if their name was not attached to it. I feel that the only failure of this project was the student's inability to address the strengths and weaknesses of the work of their peers as well as their own strengths and weaknesses in their own work. While the peer evaluations were submitted anonymously, a majority of students gave everyone "excellent" marks, when in reality it was obvious that some group members had contributed much more than others. In an effort to encourage even more anonymity, students in later classes were asked to put all of the forms into the same envelope which was then given to me, so that they knew that there was no way for me to determine who filled out which form. This approach has helped some feel comfortable giving more critical feedback. I also completed this rubric for each student based on my observations over the course of the entire project which was averaged in with the group member feedback to determine each student's final participation grade (Figure 12.1).

Rubric: Curriculum Building Project

	Excellent 4 pts	Good 3 pts	Fair 2 pts	Needs to Improve 1 pts	Unacceptable 0 pts
Listening Skills	Excellent Listens to others' ideas without interrupting; responds positively to ideas even if rejecting; asks questions about the ideas.	Good Listens to others' ideas without interrupting; responds positively to ideas even if rejecting	Fair Sometimes listens to others' ideas without interrupting; generally responds to ideas.	Needs to Improve Interrupts others' articulation of their ideas; Does not comment or makes deprecatory comments and/or gestures.	Unacceptable Never shows up and never contributes.
Contribution	Excellent Always contributes; Quality of contributions is exceptional.	Good Usually contributes; Quality of contributions is solid.	Fair Sometimes contributes; quality of contributions is fair.	Needs to Improve Rarely contributes; Quality of contributions is inconsistent or irrelevant.	Unacceptable Never contributes.
Cooperation	Excellent Group member treated others respectfully and shared the workload fairly.	Good Group member usually treated others respectfully and shared the workload fairly.	Fair Group member sometimes treated others disrespectfully or did not share the workload fairly.	Needs to Improve Group member often treated others disrespectfully or did not share the workload fairly.	Unacceptable Group member did not contribute.
Preparation	Excellent Always completes assignments; Always comes to team sessions with necessary documents/materials. Does additional research, reading, writing, designing, implementing.	Good Typically completes assignments; Typically comes to team sessions with necessary documents/materials.	Fair Sometimes completes assignments; Sometimes comes to team sessions with necessary documents/materials.	Needs to Improve Typically does not complete assignments; typically comes to team sessions without necessary documents/materials.	Unacceptable Never shows up and never contributes.
Time Management	Excellent Completed assigned tasks on time.	Good Usually completed assigned tasks on time and did not hold up progress on the projects because of incomplete work.	Fair Did not complete assigned tasks on time, and held up completion of project work.	Needs to Improve Did not complete most of the assigned tasks on time and often forced the group to make last-minute adjustments and changes to accommodate missing work.	Unacceptable Group member did not contribute.
Leadership	Excellent Group member assumed leadership in an appropriate way when necessary by helping the group stay on track, encouraging group participation, posing solutions to problems, and having a positive attitude	Good Group member sometimes assumed leadership in an appropriate way by helping the group stay on track and encouraging group participation	Fair Group member usually allowed others to assume leadership or often dominated the group	Needs to Improve Group member did not assume leadership or assumed it in a nonproductive manner.	Unacceptable Group member did not participate.

Figure 12.1 Curriculum Project Rubric

When completing any PBL project, the research gathered and the final curriculum can be very different depending on how the group approaches the problem. To address this, I created a very flexible grading rubric that focused more on the process than the final outcome. Students were graded after each of the first four sections was presented on their participation in the process and if the information gathered reflected the question asked. The final projects were graded based on overall cohesion and their utilization of the information gathered during the first four questions. This grading system worked well because it held students accountable throughout the process (Figure 12.2).

Curriculum Project Final Rubric

Name:_____

Question 1 - Group Presentation:
  ○ Relevant to Question – 10 pts.   _____

  ○ Presentation – 5 pts.   _____

Question 2 - Group Presentation:
  ○ Relevant to Question – 10 pts.   _____

  ○ Presentation – 5 pts.   _____

Question 3 - Group Presentation:
  ○ Relevant to Question – 10 pts.   _____

  ○ Presentation – 5 pts.   _____

Question 4 - Group Presentation:
  ○ Relevant to Question – 10 pts.   _____

  ○ Presentation – 5 pts.   _____

Final Project
  Group Presentation – 20 pts.   _____

  Curriculum Project

  ○ 12 Lessons – 16 pts.   _____

  ○ Reflect all gathered information – 16 pts.   _____

  ○ Cohesion – 8 pts.   _____

Group Participation Score – 30 pts.   _____

Total Points: _____/150

Figure 12.2 Curriculum Project Final Rubric

I have now run this PBL project several times and have slowly tweaked the process with each implementation. Initially, I had students report verbally on each question of the process, but I quickly determined that they needed to submit their ideas on paper so that all of the information was available for the final project. This change seems to have been beneficial for all students. We also spend more class time now than we did initially reflecting on the information during each phase of the project. This has resulted in more cohesion in the final projects because they have a better understanding of how all of the information should fit together.

In my experience, this PBL project is beneficial to the students because it teaches them how to research specific questions and use this information to create a final project that is useful. An added benefit is that they come away with a curricular unit that they can utilize in their future classrooms and the skills needed to do this again in the future. I will certainly continue to utilize this PBL problem with future classes.

Notes

1 Twachtman-Bassett, Jennifer and Diane Twachtman-Cullen. *The IEP from A to Z: How to Create Meaningful and Measurable Goals and Objectives*. San Francisco, CA: Jossey-Bass, 2011.
2 National Association for Music Educators. "Common Core Music Standards." Accessed January 17, 2018. https://nafme.org/my-classroom/standards/core-music-standards/.
3 Barbe, Walter Burke and Michael N. Milone. "What We Know about Modality Strengths". *Educational Leadership* 38, no. 5 (1981): 378–80.
4 Gardner, Howard. *Frames of Mind*. New York: Basic Book, Inc., 1983.
5 Gardner, Howard. *The Unschooled Mind: How Children Think and How Schools Should Teach*. New York: Basic Books, Inc., 1991.
6 Adamek, Mary and Alice Darrow. *Music in Special Education*. Silver Spring, MD: The American Music Therapy Association, Inc., 2010.
7 Meyer, Leila. "4 Ways Teachers Are Learning to Use Technology to Benefit Students with Special Needs." *T H E Journal* 43, no. 2 (2016): 20–23.

13

Problem-Based Learning and the Musician's Role of 'Educator' in First-Semester Aural Skills

RODNEY GARRISON

Our last case study allows us to look at the role of teaching in what most of us consider a highly skills-based subject – aural skills. In this chapter, Rodney utilizes the open-ended nature of Problem-Based Learning (PBL) to explore the possibility of adding a teaching component to his aural skills class, hoping to broaden the relevance of the subject to other music careers. Students were asked to present plans that not only incorporated class skills such as solfege or Takadimi but also included a larger component of why their chosen audience should care about music literacy in the first place. Rodney demonstrates that PBL can address this essential question which usually remains unexamined inside the music academy.

~

Music majors in the United States typically take a required sequence of music theory and aural skills/ear training courses during their freshman and sophomore years. The focus of these courses is on the acquisition and development of musical skills that involve the literacy and fluency of a variety of Western musical styles, often reaching back to the Renaissance. The overarching sameness among the bevy of music theory and aural skills textbooks is a testament to the institutionalized nature of these courses, including those offered at SUNY Fredonia, where I teach.

When assigned to teach Aural Skills 1 in the fall semester of 2017, I recalled my years of experience with the course, as well as my recent experience implementing Problem-Based Learning (PBL) in Music Appreciation (see *Heightening Music Appreciation via Problem-Based Learning* in this book). Upon reflection, I chose to explore PBL further and in a similar vein, taking care to enrich, not subvert or negate, the esteemed goals of their institutionalized models. Applying PBL to a course within an established, highly structured course sequence presents challenges that Music Appreciation and other one-semester courses with more mutable content do not. Possibly, the greatest challenge with any highly structured course is to not engage in a strategy where the benefit comes at a cost, i.e. a zero-sum game.

In addition to course content challenges, aural skills (and music theory) instructors need to create a learning environment that promotes the relevance and applicability of course content to various music careers sought by their students. As it relates to SUNY Fredonia, students studying music education, music performance, music composition, sound-recording technology, music therapy, and music industry all take aural skills for different reasons, and conveying course content as simply a list of facts and skills is not conducive to inspiring student interest, memory retention, or program retention. In short, I wanted to see if the open-ended nature of a PBL activity could both enrich the most important content of Aural Skills 1 and promote its relevance and applicability to various careers.

Every professional musician is part performer, creator, educator, collaborator, independent learner, entrepreneur, etc., at least to some degree. While students experience personal growth in some of these roles in music theory and aural skills courses, the role they generally do not explore during their first semester or even throughout the entire course sequence is that of "educator." The conventional wisdom of *"Docendo discimus"* ("By teaching, we learn"), as popularized by the Roman philosopher Seneca the Younger (*c.* 4 BC–AD 65), suggests that teaching is another learning opportunity. This chapter addresses the potential benefits and drawbacks of implementing an "educator-focused" PBL activity for Aural Skills 1 that can be shaped by students working in small teams and can be applied to any musical field. The activity was conducted across three sections of Aural Skills 1, totaling 65 graded students; it spanned the middle six and a half weeks of the 15-week semester; it was primarily completed outside the classroom, concluding with detailed activity plans that were demonstrated in class; and it was weighted as 10% of the overall course grade.

Aural Skills 1 Background Information

In Aural Skills 1 at SUNY Fredonia, students focus on the study of diatonic tonal and modal music, using movable "do" solfege, Curwen/Kodály hand signs, and the Takadimi Rhythm System. (The Takadimi Rhythm System was designed in the 1990s by Richard Hoffman, William Pelto, and John W. White as a beat-oriented system that addresses the shortcomings of both earlier beat-oriented systems and systems that emphasize counting within measures.) I consistently incorporate flipped classroom technique by devoting time for performance during class and time for learning outside the classroom. Students receive just enough performance instruction during class that they must then apply outside the classroom in order to learn assigned melodies and rhythms to be performed in a subsequent class. If students require further review of newly acquired skills, my office hours are available, upperclassman tutors are available, and online learning materials are supplied in advance and used as needed. I also incorporate traditional homework assignments that test the ability to analyze and notate dictated musical ideas that are both rehearsed during class and outside the classroom as needed. I encourage students to collaborate with each other when working on any skill outside the classroom, as there are plenty of solo written and oral testing opportunities during class.

In total, all mentioned and unmentioned course activities leave no room for the student musician to develop the role of "educator." Instructors may not choose to take time from a literacy and fluency building course – much less the first semester of such a course – to explore the development of this role. The issues of time, skill level, and content specificity are well received; however, they can all be mediated by PBL to some degree. Perhaps students can have all the benefits of a beginning aural skills course while exploring the "educator" role, a role that can strengthen learning. In addition to strengthening knowledge specific to the course, I hoped that students, while working in small teams, would learn more about their own desired musical career and the potentially different desired musical careers of their teammates and classmates. Sharing of expertise is one of the most significant components of PBL group work.

Aural Skills 1 PBL Activity (PBLA) Instructions and Details

The PBLA instructions described an open-ended activity for small groups, tasking them to teach some aspect of both Movable Do Solfege and the Takadimi Rhythm System to audiences of their choosing. While open-ended, group activities are a hallmark of PBL, this activity includes a more specific design that, like a project, steers the groups toward defined and at least moderately controlled goals. In essence, this PBLA is a hybrid between Problem- and Project-based learning. I designed the PBLA this way because I wanted to keep students focused on course content while also giving them some freedom with how they choose use course content. Here are the PBLA instructions and accompanying sections:

PBL Instructions

    In teams of three, create two activity plans: one for teaching Movable Do Solfege in some capacity and the other for teaching the Takadimi Rhythm System in some capacity. As a team, you decide the type of audience you would like to educate for each activity, and you design the lessons accordingly. Your two activities may not have the same audience, and plan each activity to last for 20 minutes in real time. Your team will also create and perform a five-minute demonstration of each activity on an assigned day and time. There is a fair amount of paperwork to create and complete in order to document your team and individual work, so please read "The Details" and subsequent sections thoroughly. All documents needed have been made available on OnCourse (a Google course management system).

The Details

You may choose any type of audience you want, so use your interests and creativity. (Example: If you want to share Takadimi with retirees, then your audience for that activity could be retirement home residents that may or may not have some musical background. Additionally, if you wish, your classmates can pretend to be any audience for the duration of your five-minute demonstration.)

Teams of three have been assigned at random, and your demonstration date and time have also been assigned. Each member of the team must have a nearly equal part in both activities. Please check the team rosters on OnCourse for this information. (Musicians are accustomed to not having the luxury of choosing with whom they work, so please honor your teammates and refrain from requesting reassignment. You are expected to work with each other's schedules, and you have been given about six weeks to make and execute plans. No extensions will be given, so plan accordingly.)

As a team, you will plan both activities, create an Activity Plan for both activities, and provide transcribed music (notate the melody, bass line, or outer voices if the piece has two or more voices) for all music used in both Activity Plans and demonstrations. If there are lyrics involved with the music, you must transcribe them as well. All teammates will participate in both five-minute demonstrations. Your demonstrations may make use of the technology provided in your classroom, technology you have or can borrow, as well as any instrument you have, can borrow, or can create. (You would be wise to create a plan for your demonstrations. The quality of your demonstrations will be reflected in your grade.)

As an individual, you will fill out a Team and Self-Assessment, a questionnaire that is due on Monday, November 6. Among other things, the questionnaire will indicate the role each person played in each activity. Again, each member of the team must have a nearly equal part in both activities. (Example: If one of the three members does not have a large role in one area of an activity, then they should have a large role in another area of that same activity.)

Use materials, sources, instruments, and other resources you have, find, borrow, or create. Nothing is off limits. Talk to anyone that has related and valuable experience. You will need to ask a lot of questions in order to solve any and all problems. (A route to consider as you work with your team: Communicate with each other often. Use your imagination. Research. Propose Ideas. Research some more. Plan your activity. Prepare your materials. Plan your demonstration. Rehearse. Refine everything to make it the best it can be.)

Make sure you keep track of the documents you create. Losing an unsaved document from this or any other step in this process is not an excuse for needing an extension. Make use of shared Google Docs and the like.

Documenting Sources for the Activity Plans:
Create footnotes in your document for every idea, source, document, video, recording, etc. that you did not create, so that your documentation will lead others to find your sources. For each item, you must provide the following information and in the order listed:

1. Author(s) and or performer(s) names, as well as the editor if credited
   (Point of quality control: If there is no author, or you cannot find one, then do not use the source.)
2. Title of the source, idea, document, video, recording, etc.
   (If an article or chapter, then also include the journal or book title.)
3. Publishing company and/or website, whichever is necessary
4. Date of publication if the source is not a web-based source or date of access if the source is a web-based source
   If your Activity Plan has no footnotes, your grade will reflect your refusal to properly document your sources (Table 13.1).

Items Due on Your Specified Demonstration Day (either October 30 or November 1):

1. A printed copy of your detailed Activity Plan for movable "do" solfege that includes transcribed music (notate the melody, bass line, or outer voices if the piece has two or more voices) for all music used. (One copy per team is required.)
2. A printed copy of your detailed Activity Plan for the Takadimi Rhythm System that includes transcribed music (notate the melody, bass line, or outer voices if the piece has two or more voices) for all music used. (One copy per team is required.)

Item Due on Monday, November 6:
Each person will turn in a printed copy of the Team and Self-Assessment. (The questionnaire be typed using Word, Google Docs, or some other reliable word processing program.)

Table 13.1 PBL Activity Plan Layout

Activity Plan Layout:

Each of the two activity plans must contain the following items and must be created on a recent word processing program, such as Word or Google Doc (that you can all edit!):

1. State the title of your activity, as well as the names of all three teammates.
2. Define your audience and their anticipated level of musical experience. (Be realistic and spare no details on this or any step to follow.)
3. List three reasons why your audience should care about music literacy. (Perhaps not every audience should care about music literacy for the same reasons. If the reason is not original to the team, remember to footnote it.)
4. Define your 20-minute activity in a precise and methodical way. (Explain what are you going to do in either prose or a step-by-step list. You will need multiple sentences/steps to explain the activity well. Anyone reading this should be able to follow and recreate every step of the activity –like a really thoughtful recipe. You may need a footnote or two.)
5. Define the objectives of your activity in a clear and thoughtful manner. (Explain what you want the audience to gain from your activity. Assume you need several sentences to do so. You may need a footnote or two.)
6. List the tools/resources needed for your activity. (If using sources, videos, recordings, etc. that were not created by you, you will certainly need footnotes.)
7. Explain the benefits of this activity – there should be more than one – and how you think you will know if your audience is experiencing them. What are your expectations of the audience, keeping in mind that not all audiences will respond or be expected to respond in the same ways? (Again, a short or pithy answer will not do the job.)

- If using Word, simply download the .doc file and open in Word
- If using Google Docs, simply download the .doc file, sign in to Google Docs, start a new, blank document, click on File, click on Open, click on Upload, and then select the .doc file or drag the .doc file into the delineated area
- Make sure you keep track of the documents you create. Losing an unsaved document from this or any other step in this process is not an excuse for needing an extension.

Aural Skills 1 PBLA Team and Self-Assessment Instructions and Details

After giving in-class demonstrations of their activity plans, students completed a Team and Self-Assessment questionnaire that, as stated above, was due either five or seven days after their demonstrations. The assessment was designed to help me know how involved each student was in the creation of both activity plans and their demonstrations. It also served to motivate students to hold themselves and their teammates accountable for their actions, as the PBLA was largely created outside the classroom. In order to promote independent work on the assessment, the instructions included the following guideline: "If you provide the same answers as another student, you and the other student will not earn credit for this assignment." The assessment questions are listed in Table 13.2.

Table 13.2 PBL Assessment Questions

Assessment Questions:

1. Were you resistant to keeping up with the suggested work schedule? If so, why? If not, why not?
2. Was anyone on the team resistant to keeping up with the suggested work schedule? If so, why? If not, why not? (Be specific regarding teammate names and actions.)
3. Did you make a suggestion for an activity plan that was either accepted or rejected by the team? Tell me about this experience and why you think your activity idea was accepted or rejected.
4. What did you contribute to the **solfege activity plan**? (Be specific.)
5. What did each of your teammates contribute to the **solfege activity plan**? (Be specific regarding teammate names and actions.)
6. During the creation of the **solfege activity plan**, how could you have contributed more to your group, and why do you think this may be helpful? (or) If you could not have contributed more to your group, how could you have helped someone else in your group without doing work for them? (or) If everything was well balanced, please explain what that experience was like. (Be specific regarding teammate names and actions.)
7. What did you contribute to the **Takadimi activity plan**? (Be specific.)
8. What did each of your teammates contribute to the **Takadimi activity plan**? (Be specific regarding teammate names and actions.)
9. During the creation of the **Takadimi activity plan**, how could you have contributed more to your group, and why do you think this may be helpful? (or) If you could not have contributed more to your group, how could you have helped someone else in your group without doing work for them? (or) If everything was well balanced, please explain what that experience was like. (Be specific regarding teammate names and actions.)
10. Thinking back on this team experience, how did you respond to contributions offered or not offered by others in your group? (Be specific regarding teammate names and actions.)
11. Thinking back on this team experience, how did your teammates respond to contributions offered or not offered by you? (Be specific regarding teammate names and actions.)
12. Describe your emotional experience working on the PBLA; i.e. describe the possible fluctuation of your motivation level and your emotional responses to the tasks at hand.

(Continued)

Table 13.2 Continued

13. In order to make room in the course plan for your PBLA, two of your Contextual Listening homework assignments (each a highly directed, small project) were omitted. Now that you have completed the PBLA, think about how you feel about this decision. If you had some control over the course content, would you rather: (A) have two more Contextual Listening homework assignments instead of the PBLA, (B) have a PBLA instead of another two Contextual Listening homework assignments, or (C) not make this kind of decision because you do not prefer one activity over the other?
14. Reflection: What is your overall appraisal of this PBLA? Was it successful, unsuccessful, or both? Please explain your thoughts.

Aural Skills 1 PBLA Implementation

The PBLA was conducted across three sections of Aural Skills 1, initially involving 71 students that were sorted within their respective sections into a total of 23 teams. Of the 23 teams, 21 were three-member teams and two were four-member teams. Six students withdrew from Aural Skills 1 over the six-and-a-half-week time span, affecting the population of some teams without decreasing the total number of teams. At the end of the PBLA, there were 17 three-member teams, 1 four-member team, and 5 two-member teams. With only one exception, I did not reassign teams as students withdrew, even though this resulted in five teams with only two members, in order to avoid disrupting previous teamwork. Students were sorted into teams alphabetically, which proved to be a desired, random sorting, as last names do not consider student relationships, majors, levels of talent or skill, or work ethic. The following list states the different majors represented by the 65 graded students, from the greatest representation to the least:

- 36 (55%) BM Music Education majors
- 10 (15%) BS Music Therapy majors
- 9 (14%) BS Sound Recording Technology, BS Music Industry, or BA Applied Music majors
- 6 (9%) BM Performance majors
- 4 (6%) BM Composition majors.

The PBLA was assigned at the beginning of the fifth week of the 15-week semester. By then, students had experience sightsinging with movable "do" solfege in major and minor contexts, using Curwen/Kodály hand signs in major and minor contexts, and performing melodies and rhythms in simple and compound meters using the Takadimi Rhythm System. They also had some experience with transcribing major and minor melodies and bass lines, as well as rhythms in simple and compound meters. All of these skills were potentially used in the development of their activity plans, and skills were

Table 13.3 PBL Suggested Work Schedule

Suggested Work Schedule:
• Week 1: Create a team email thread using your Fredonia Gmail accounts, communicate schedules with each other, and create meeting times. Create an activity idea for both solfege and Takadimi on your own to suggest to the team in the second week.
• Week 2: Individually suggest activity ideas, and, as a team, choose the best two plans for research and development. Create and use shared Google Docs to document work.
• Week 3 and 4: Research, develop, and communicate to build and strengthen your two activity plans.
• Week 5: Formally document your activity plans.
• Week 6: Create and rehearse your activity plan demonstrations.
• Between Week 6 and your performance day, refine and finalize your work as needed.

strengthened during the PBLA time span through continued study inside and outside the classroom. As the activity plans and their demonstrations were primarily completed outside the classroom, students were provided with a suggested work schedule, as provided in Table 13.3.

As time went on, students were given a few in-class prompts and emails to remind them of where they should be at a given time. Teams affected by student withdrawal or nonparticipation were advised as soon as possible. In total, six students withdrew from the course, and four students chose not to participate in any meaningful way. Teams with students who did not participate were simply advised to keep working and documenting their progress.

Around week five, I received emails about two topics that warranted a mass clarification for all teams. The first topic involved the third step of the Activity Plan Layout, which read, "List three reasons why your audience should care about music literacy." While offering clarification, I upheld distinctions between "should" in the third step, "objectives" in the fifth step, and "benefits" in the seventh step was crucial. Here is the summary of my response: describing why your audience should care about music literacy is giving thought to how you can help them enrich future musical experiences through an activity that is closely related to how they currently experience music, or, depending on the desires, needs, and abilities of your audience, through an activity that is unrelated to how they currently experience music. Describing your objectives is essentially making a summary of how your audience will participate in this enriching music experience, and this summary follows and is closely related to the detailed, step-by-step plan that precedes it. Describing the benefits of your activity is a detailing of the new or strengthened skills and experiences that your activity promotes. These three steps were meant to inspire students to connect with research on a level deeper than simply borrowing activity ideas from others, as they create a narrative that fosters a cohesion of ideas, process, and results.

The second topic involved clarification of what students could do to make the most of their five-minute, in-class demonstration of each activity plan. My suggestions were based on the ideas that their classmates did not need to be taught the course material, and they would act as the audience defined in the plan. In other words, demonstrations were best spent on participation and not lecture, as the following two circumstances illustrate: if your plan builds to a main activity, then the most efficient thing to do is to state the intended audience, summarize the main activity, and then use the remaining minutes to engage the class in the main activity. If your plan is more evenly divided across, say, three activities, then, after the audience statement, the class could participate in micro demonstrations of at least two of those activities. I also suggested that the demonstration should mirror an overall purpose of the plan, in that it should communicate whether the plan is designed to teach a new skill(s) or contribute to a deeper understanding of a preexisting skill(s).

Students were not made aware of the exact grading rubric during the PBLA, although they were aware that the PBLA was weighted as 10% of the overall course grade and that the bulk of their grade would not come from the Team and Self-Assessment. The grading rubric with values expressed as points that add up to 100 is presented in Table 13.4.

Table 13.4 PBL Final Grading Plan Rubric

I. Activity Plan Total = 60 (two 30-point activity plans)

Movable Do Solfege plan total = 30	Takadimi Rhythm System plan total = 30
#2 Define audience = 4	#2 Define audience = 4
#3 Why the audience should care = 4	#3 Why the audience should care = 4
#4 20-minute plan details = 10	#4 20-minute plan details = 10
#5 Objectives stated = 4	#5 Objectives stated = 4
#6 Documentation = 4	#6 Documentation = 4
#7 Benefits stated = 4	#7 Benefits stated = 4

II. Demonstration Total = 20
Quality of word choice/delivery = 5
Organization between speakers = 5
Adequate examples = 5
Time management/flow = 5

III. Team and Self-Assessment Total = 20
Each question was worth one point, and the remaining points were reserved to be subtracted for errors in formatting, grammar, and otherwise not following instructions.

Aural Skills 1 PBLA Activity Plan and Demonstration Outcomes

The 23 teams created a total of 23 Movable Do Solfege activity plans and 23 Takadimi Rhythm System activity plans. The following list states the different audiences that students identified for solfege plans, from the greatest representation to the least:

- 12 (52%): K–12 public school education (5 for elementary school, 4 for middle school, and 3 for high school)
- 6 (26%): adults with little to no background in music
- 2 (9%): children who are not in K–12 public school education
- 2 (9%): adult, nonprofessional musicians
- 1 (4%): children in a special education program.

The following list states the different audiences that students identified for Takadimi plans, from the greatest representation to the least:

- 19 (83%): K–12 public school education (8 for elementary school, 4 for middle school, and 7 for high school)
- 3 (13%): adult, nonprofessional musicians
- 1 (4%): music therapy.

As compared to the previously recorded major demographics, the plan topics skewed toward BM Music Education majors. Also considering how most students at SUNY Fredonia students were educated in K–12 public schools, the topic statistics are not surprising.

In the activity plans, incorporating some prior experience is logical and expected. Over reliance upon prior experience with little reliance on present research manifested in the following three negative ways: making generalizations regarding musical selections that "everyone knows" in order to save instruction time without considering another way to achieve the same goals; making inappropriate musical choices, such as using a children's song with an older, unrelated audience; and avoiding the use of musical jargon, instead choosing to talk around the very concept they should name. For example, more than one team planned a solfege activity around experiencing modulation without mentioning the word "modulation" in the activity plan or the demonstration. While most activity plans adequately documented music sources, and many documented ideas used in rationalizations of "why your audience should care about music literacy" and "benefits of your activity," most lacked documentation of activity ideas, suggesting a lack of research conducted in steps four and five of the plan. Overall, teams needed to research activities suited for specific audiences more. Additionally, about half of the teams needed to add more details to their plans, as well as pay more attention to grammar.

Interestingly, the teams chose activities that did not rely on technology, with the exception of equipment needed to play music recordings or project a shared musical example. Most props, if props were used, were instruments, large signs, or small items that require or elicit physical participation. The majority of the activities were wisely designed for total audience participation. A few activities were designed to engage only a few audience members at a time, which left others unoccupied and unengaged. Students quickly realized that all of their activity design choices, especially the ones they seemed less confident about, affected their demonstrations. Those who did not communicate well with each other, lacked detail in their activity plan, and/or lacked research in their activity plan were the ones who needed more work with word choice and/or had the most difficulties with transitions between speakers and pacing of the demonstration. Without fail, every person who either chose not to participate in a meaningful way or chose to participate less than other teammates became apparent in the demonstration and/or the Team and Self-Assessment.

Despite the focus on the negative outcomes of the PBLA in this section, there were numerous positive outcomes. During the research and development weeks of the PBLA, students handled team changes, in-class discussions, and email correspondence quite well. The majority of students had positive and energetic attitudes during their activity plan demonstrations, and they were genuinely open to participate with and learn from other teams. Every team was prepared to present on the day and time assigned, and every team handed in all materials due at that time.

Aural Skills 1 PBLA Team and Self-Assessment Outcomes

The Team and Self-Assessment was available to students early on in the PBLA process, even though it was not due until about a week after the PBLA demonstrations. I encouraged students to read the questions but answer them only after the demonstrations. All questions, save the final two, were designed to reinforce the way students were instructed to work within a team by requiring students to record many of their personal and interpersonal experiences. Although dependent upon the level of honesty offered, answers indicated how well students and their teammates functioned. Combined with my demonstration observations, I was able to determine a fairly accurate summary of team dynamics and activity. It was possible for information within assessments to affect one's overall PBLA grade and not just the assessment portion of the grade. If teammates identified an unnecessary and avoidable problem caused by a member who did not contribute in equal measure, then points were deducted from the overall PBLA grade of that member. Normal and expected situations like personality differences, differences in opinion, and varying experience levels did not generate grade deductions. Of the 65 graded students, 60 turned in a completed assessment. Of the five students that did

not turn in an assessment, four were the same students who did not participate in the PBLA in any meaningful way.

The final two questions of the assessment asked students to assess the PBLA
itself. Having experienced both the PBLA and Contextual Listening homework assignments earlier in the semester, Question 13 asked students for their
retrospective, hypothetical preference of assignment among three choices: (A)
have two more Contextual Listening homework assignments instead of the
PBLA, (B) have a PBLA instead of another two Contextual Listening homework assignments, or (C) not make this kind of decision because you do not
prefer one activity over the other. Of the 60 responses, 17 (28%) students chose
A, 32 (53%) students chose B, and 11 (19%) students chose C. Question 14
asked students to state their overall appraisal of the PBLA as successful, unsuccessful, or both, with the addition of comments. Of the 60 responses, 40
(67%) students thought the PBLA was successful, 6 (10%) students thought the
PBLA was unsuccessful, and 14 (23%) students thought the PBLA was both
successful and unsuccessful. As anticipated, comments were generally a combination of their appraisal of the PBLA design and their actual team experience. Only one repetitive comment stood out: several students felt that BM
Music Education majors benefited the most from the PBLA. None of the students who left this comment followed it with any further explanation. While
I do not know if they thought the PBLA was expressly designed to benefit BM
Music Education majors, giving little consideration to the other majors, I did
not attempt to design the PBLA to benefit one major over the others.

Aural Skills 1 PBLA Assessment and Conclusion

Within any level of aural skills, there is a general, recurring cycle of learning new performance skills and then rehearsing those skills. The PBLA was
not designed to teach students new performance skills; it was designed for
students to rehearse and strengthen recently learned skills, while also applying them to self-determined educational opportunities that aligned with their
musical interests. The PBLA supplemented the more traditional means of rehearsal happening in the classroom; it was not a substitution for them. While
six and a half weeks seems like a long review period, I had to factor in all of the
other courses, activities, and performances happening outside the classroom.
I decided I would rather err on the side of too much time to complete the
PBLA as opposed to too little time because research and creativity suffer when
time is lacking. There was also no reason why new performance skills could
not be introduced in the classroom during this time, as the PBLA was not the
primary focus of the class.

I support the idea of having three members per team. An odd number of
teammates as opposed to an even number seems conducive to promoting an
equal division of labor across the two activity plans, which was a primary

goal of the group work. I believe teams of five would be too large, and if I could have avoided teams of two, I would have. There are a few things I would change about the PBLA: I would be more specific about requiring different sources to be included in multiple steps of the activity plan, specifically where students explain their activity and its objectives in steps four and five of the activity plan. To aid students in this research effort, I would supply them with a sample list of websites and journals for different musical fields that are accessible to them online and/or through the university library. In order to combat the notion that BM Music Education majors benefit the most from the PBLA, I would provide students with a sample audience related to each major. I believe students should continue to develop the skill of being creative with knowledge as soon as knowledge is acquired. I also hope to enlighten students to see how relevant the acquisition of aural skills is to all musical endeavors as early in their studies as possible, attempting to create a lasting and positive influence as they continue on in the aural skills sequence and their musical career.

Conclusion

14
Best Practices for Problem-Based Learning in the College Music Classroom

NATALIE SARRAZIN

The major goal of this volume was to introduce readers to Problem-based Learning (PBL) in the college music classroom through a wide range of case studies that demonstrate its potential. The instigating factor behind this project was that while this approach has been successful in other subject areas for decades, it has been slow to enter the field of music, particularly at the college or university level. The case studies, which work their way through issues and successes – some anticipated and others rather surprising – illustrate creative solutions, student feedback, practical organizational strategies, and tools useful for implementing PBL in a college-level music course.

As previously mentioned, the application of PBL originated in science-based classrooms – typical in medicine. Known for problem-solving and active, engaged learning, PBL's success inspired other fields to follow suit, eventually trickling down to the K–12 music classrooms. And while its implementation there may be due to a more professional development-minded teaching staff who are required to keep up to date with advances in the latest pedagogical techniques, K–12 also illustrates a certain level of adaptability of the PBL approach. The effectiveness of PBL at this level, however, still remains to be qualified regardless of its pervasiveness.

Advantages of PBL Approach

In higher education, the lecture format in music classes, particularly music history and theory, still dominates. Reasons for this include professors being rooted in the traditional pervasiveness of the lecture for certain courses (e.g. music history, music theory), and perhaps a lack of demonstrated acceptance of and effectiveness of other methods. What attracted instructors to the PBL approach was the promise of increased student engagement – engagement that introduced students to life outside of the classroom through problem-solving, teamwork, and as a more sophisticated and complex alternative to requiring only "right" or "correct" answers. When done properly, PBLs allow students to take incredible journeys into the subject matter, that, much like arts integration, brings out nuances and connections in the material that conventional teaching often misses. Nicely, Chapter 7, for example, utilized PBL when she discovered the large disconnect between the importance of music in the lives of students in her ethnomusicology class and understanding the music of others. They knew the role music played in their lives but were unable to see that same importance in music of other cultures.

PBL Implementation in Music Courses

While some of the conclusions here are general in nature, others are music-specific. Subject-specific conclusions address music's sub-disciplines such as applied, theoretical, humanities-based, and performance-based. Some instructors, such as Sarrazin, Chapter 11 and Wilcox, Chapter 10, ensconced their PBL into interdisciplinary courses, while most others sought a straight-forward theoretical or area-based approach. One question that emerged is how could the interdisciplinary approach work with the PBL. What were the issues? Was the PBL enhanced or detracted by the presence of interdisciplinarity? Despite the added "complexity" of movement, or other art forms, the PBLs were just as effective with the inclusion of interdisciplinarity. Issues that resonate in particular with Music PBLs concern, as Hunter mentions, collaboration on stage doesn't necessarily translate into PBL type collaboration.

For this volume, PBLs were implemented in all types of course formats – hybrid, undergraduate lower and upper, general education, and specialty courses; using different music sub-specialties (ethnomusicology, history, education, theory, appreciation, and movement); and in PBLs came in all forms, shapes, and sizes. Instructors put in varying amounts of effort, some such as Webb and others did major rewrites to their curriculum, while others did very little in this respect. Garrison, for example, created detailed and explicit instructions on the project/problem set up, and attempted to use the PBL to expand upon the existing traditional conservatory curriculum. In addition, Garrison employed PBL to explore entirely new dimensions of learning, such as introducing education plans in an aural skills class – something rarely done. Most instructors such as Wanamaker and Nicely broke down their PBLs into smaller, multipart sections with 3–4 shorter assignments accomplished mostly in groups, but sometimes individually, with students completing some of the work on their own before leading up to the final group PBL question. Other groups were given all of the work up front and expected to create their own timelines for completion.

PBL flexibility extended to covering the wide range of sub-disciplines. For example, due to their outcome-driven curricula, the more skill-based or performance-oriented classes such as music theory or music education leaned toward implementing *Project*-based Learning, whereas courses such as Music Appreciation, History, and Ethnomusicology were able to implement Problem-based designs. As discussed at length in various case studies in this volume, Project and Problem-based Learning are relatively identical, with the caveat being the form of the final project or outcome. For example, Horsington's music theory course, Wilcox's introduction to music course, and Wanamaker and Sarrazin's music education classes required specific outcomes within a restricted format and curricula that requires detailed step-by-step and hands-on instruction. As a result, their "projects" were less open-ended than those in more theoretical courses in the humanities such as ethnomusicology or history. The instructors developed solutions that fit their course needs – either be creating a straight Project-based design or finding an "interstitial" solution, splitting both Problem- and Project-based approaches down the middle to create a hybrid Problem-/Project-based activity.

It is safe to say that given this information, it might be difficult to achieve a fully transformative change in the college music curricula across all sub-disciplines, and PBLs may be relegated to remain as course-based activities.

Methods of Curricular Adoption Implementation

One of the main decisions that faced authors was how to organize and manage the PBL. All instructors started with similar questions which were centered around curriculum and time. How can I implement this into my existing, already full curriculum? How can I provide students with enough time to thoroughly conduct the PBL in the class? Outside? Most instructors started the PBL very early in the semester, while others waited until later on in the semester. Deadlines for group work deposits along the way were another issue, as was how much oversight to give. Instructors offered a variety of solutions for introducing their PBLs. Some introduced the PBL early on in the semester. Garrison, in an effort to curtail the end of semester rush, encouraged students to read the PBL assessment early in the semester to plan ahead. Those that introduced their PBL too late in the semester regretted it by the end and would definitely move up the instruction on the PBL. Others found creative ways of embedding it deeper into the curriculum and give students more out-of-class time. Hunter, Chapter 7, for example, encouraged use of her social media and asked that students not only write a paper on "What is PBL?" but also participate in chat groups on Facebook, and meet virtually over Skype or Google Hangouts. Many of her students chose to use these platforms to complete their projects.

PBLs work in both positive and negative ways. For example, while many instructors found that they continually needed to refocus the students through in-class or drop box interventions, almost everyone realized the value of increasing the flexibility in their classroom around the PBL, such as adding lectures or PBL discussion where needed, and using PBL for teachable moments and tangents. Hunter points out that instructors need to be prepared for the "transparency of the research project" that enables student reflexivity on the production of knowledge.

Given the importance of assessment and accountability in higher education, PBLs must fit into existing course goals and Student Learning Objectives (SLOs). While most authors adjusted their PBL to accommodate their existing SLOs, others, such as Wanamaker in Chapter 12, created SLOs just to assess this project.

Hunter, meanwhile, realized that the "PBL framework can be incorporated through both ongoing day-to-day modes of inquiry and interaction in the classroom, as well as larger-scale research projects that span the semester," thus implying the use of PBL as pedagogical tool on two levels of inquiry.

For instructors such as Hunter, the implementation of research and creativity were important ones. Hunter, in an effort to insert a balance of research, required students to provide eight sources grounded in research rather than relying solely on the creative.

The Challenges of Group Work

Most of the larger issues with PBLs had little to do with music, but rather concerned the nature of group format. Student complaints focused on the idea of group work in general – mostly seen as an unfair or less effective pedagogical method to begin with. The main complaint was "fair grading" and the notion that each student would earn a separate grade rather than one grade for the entire group.

Several surprising results can be embodied by the "grass is always greener" sentiment. In Wanamaker's class, for example, she found bias in perceptions of classroom behaviors based on the processes of the PBL project. Students in Garrison's class who were not music majors felt that the PBL was geared toward music majors and therefore favored them, while the music majors felt that the nonmusic majors benefited!

Another issue was group member selection. Students selecting their own groups create imbalances, and students denied the freedom to create their own groups complain that they would have been better off with friends due to "schedule conflicts." These points are valid to an extent; however, the point of group work is to function with other people, learn to cooperate, collaborate, etc. with *any* people, not only ones that you know. Schedules will get in the way any time you have more than one person involved, and overcoming them is one of the challenges that colleagues face in the real world every single day. Some PBLs, as reported by Nicely, Chapter 7, found that students, once immersed in the project, overcame much of their resistance to group work. This was not the case for everyone, however, and other instructors sought to actively mediate concerns over many aspects of group work implementation.

Hunter, in Chapter 8, directly addressed work distribution In order to facilitate greater individual accountability and group equity, it might be helpful for students to engage in ongoing individual reflection on their role, and the interactions and work of the group. This could be factored into their class participation grade.

Others, such as Wanamaker, Chapter 12, and Garrison, Chapters 13 and 5, took more stalwart approaches, with the philosophy that "this is the real world" and imposed a system of group division without student input. In either case, students have to complete the exact same activities, from assigning tasks to producing a final product, and in the real world, you have very little input on who your team consists of. As Garrison notes in his assignment directions, "Musicians are accustomed to not having the luxury of choosing with whom they work, so please honor your teammates and refrain from requesting reassignment. You are expected to work with each other's schedules, and you have been given about six weeks to make and execute plans. No extensions will be given, so plan accordingly."

Conclusion

The case studies offered here provide only a glimpse – a beginning foray, if you will, into the PBL pedagogical approach, but hopefully one that leaves the reader with an understanding of its potential for student engagement in higher education music courses.

As is evidenced by the lessons presented here, the authors demonstrate that PBL is not only "doable" but advantageous to music classes in a variety of sub-disciplines – from Music Appreciation, Music Theory, History, Ethnomusicology, Therapy, and Education. What these chapters demonstrate is the range of courses in which PBL approach might be implemented – upper and lower divisions, major and nonmajor, descriptions of processes of implementation, assessment techniques and rubrics, and how PBLs might fit into existing curricula given the current student learning outcomes.

As John Thomerson correctly points out in Chapter 3, the case studies presented here are preliminary in that they do not transform the pedagogical base for the course, but rather remain part of the didactic curriculum (Savery, 14). While this is certainly true, the case studies do represent a starting point designed to provide basic information, processes, and criteria by which one can ascertain the practicality of applying the approach in college music courses. Unfortunately, it will take many more years of PBL application in college music courses before it moves beyond didactic teaching. Only then can it be implemented toward large-scale curricular reform, although this may never be so for certain types of skill- or performance-based music courses. In the meantime, however, a review of these case studies will provide some insight into future application and hopefully, can be used to correct, amplify, and strengthen them.

Reference

For good introductions to PBL, see David H. Jonassen and Woei Hung, "Problem-based Learning," In *Encyclopedia of the Sciences of Learning*, edited by WHO. Heidelberg: Springer, 2012, 2687–90; Andrew Walker, Heather Leary, Cindy Hmelo-Silver, and Peggy A. Ertmer, eds., *Essential Readings in Problem-Based Learning: Exploring and Extending the Legacy of Howard S. Barrows*. West Lafayette, IN: Purdue University Press, 2015; and Allyn Walsh, *The Tutor in PBL: A Novice's Guide*. Hamilton, ON: McMaster University, 2005.

List of Contributors

Rodney Garrison holds two MM degrees from East Carolina University, one in music theory and the other in vocal pedagogy and performance, and a PhD in music theory from the University at Buffalo (SUNY). He has taught music theory, aural skills, and music history courses at SUNY Fredonia, as well as the University at Buffalo and Buffalo State (SUNY).

Merryl Goldberg, PhD is a Professor in the School of Arts at California State University San Marcos and Executive Director of Center ARTES. Her publications include the books *Arts Integration: Teaching Subject Matter through the Arts in Multicultural Settings* (5th edition, Routledge), *Teaching English Language Learners through the Arts: A SUAVE Experience* (2004, Allyn and Bacon), and *Arts as Education* (1992, Harvard Educational Review).

Scott Horsington, MM, MPA teaches Music Theory, World Music, and Introduction to Music at The College at Brockport. He also directs the Brockport College-Community Orchestra and Brockport Concert Band and serves as the Music Studies Ensembles Coordinator.

Julie Hunter, PhD holds a doctorate from Brown University and teaches ethnomusicology at Potsdam's Crane School of Music, specializing in the music of West Africa.

Margaret Leenhouts, DMA is a member of the Rochester Philharmonic Orchestra as well as a faculty member at Nazareth College and The College at Brockport. She holds degrees from the Eastman School of Music, the Mannes College of Music, and Yale University.

Tiffany Nicely is a percussionist and music theorist specializing in musics of West Africa and the Diaspora. She teaches World Music Cultures, Sub-Saharan African Music and Cultures, and directs the West African Drumming Ensemble at SUNY Buffalo State College.

Natalie Sarrazin, PhD teaches in the Department Theatre and Music Studies and Arts for Children program at The College at Brockport, SUNY. In addition, she is co-founder and Executive Director of Western Music Education Association, a National Association for Music Education (NAfME) affiliate in India.

John Thomerson recently completed his doctoral degree at the University of Cincinnati College-Conservatory of Music. His dissertation explored parody as a borrowing technique in contemporary American music.

Tracy S. Wanamaker, MSEd, MT-BC is a Visiting Instructor at the Crane School of Music, SUNY Potsdam, where she coordinates the Music in Special Education Program. In addition to her duties at Crane, she has a thriving music therapy private practice in Northern New York.

Gavin Webb, PhD is formally a Visiting Assistant Professor in Ethnomusicology at Binghamton University and currently the Director of International Programs at Marist College. He holds a BMus from Berklee College of Music, and an MA and PhD from the University of Ghana. Gavin has devoted 20 years of his life to studying and researching music in West Africa.

Tamara Wilcox, MM is a full-time faculty member in the Department of Theatre and Music Studies at SUNY The College at Brockport, where she teaches advanced piano, Women in Music, and Music and Healing. Tamara has a degree in collaborative piano in dance.

Index

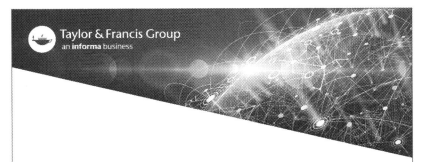

Printed in the United States
by Baker & Taylor Publisher Services